Living in China

Living in China

ANDREW WATSON

1977

LITTLEFIELD, ADAMS & CO.
Totowa, New Jersey

For Maggie, David and James

Paperback edition published 1977 by
LITTLEFIELD, ADAMS & CO.

Hardbound edition published 1975 by
ROWMAN AND LITTLEFIELD

Library of Congress Cataloging in Publication Data

Watson, Andrew J
   Living in China

   (A Littlefield, Adams Quality Paperback No. 327)
   Bibliography: p.
   Includes index.
   1. China—Description and travel—1949-
2. Watson, Andrew J.   I. Title.
[DS711.W33 1977]   951.05   76-50082
ISBN 0-8226-0327-6

PRINTED IN .THE UNITED STATES OF AMERICA

CONTENTS

PREFACE

My main goal in writing this book has been to describe as accurately as possible the life of the ordinary man in China. Although it is impossible not to use words which imply approval or disapproval, I have tried to avoid making sweeping value judgements about the nature of Chinese society. An intelligent reader is capable of deciding for himself what he likes and dislikes about another society. However, he can only do so on the basis of knowledge of what it is really like. He must first gain some idea of what China means to the Chinese in terms of their traditions, their problems and their hopes. He will then be in a position to understand the value of the society for its citizens. Hopefully, this book will provide some of that understanding.

My own attitude towards China is, on the whole, a favourable one. When they came to power in 1949, the Chinese Communists faced immense problems. Yet they have succeeded in giving the Chinese back a sense of unity, purpose and national pride. They have taken great strides along the road of social reform and industrialization. They have also achieved a great deal of social justice in terms of the distribution of wealth and privilege. Nevertheless, it would be foolish to argue that all is fine and that these things have been done without cost. Nor has everything that the Communist Party attempted been wholeheartedly welcomed by the ordinary man. There have been failures and there are still weaknesses and problems. Not least among the costs have been the political and intellectual restrictions that have enabled the Party to mobilize people to work for the immediate needs of the country. However, the opinions and reservations of a foreigner are in many ways irrelevant. What matters is what the Chinese themselves want. And whatever their own reservations, there can be no doubt that the majority are prepared to accept the goals and policies of their present political leaders.

A book of this kind owes a great debt to all people studying and writing about China. I have relied on their ideas and researches to a great extent and I hope they will forgive me for not being able to acknowledge them directly when writing. I am also indebted to the Chinese people and friends I have met during my visits to their country, in particular my former colleagues at Sian Foreign

Languages Institute. The knowledge I have gained from them has given me insights into Chinese society that would otherwise be unavailable. For their valuable comments and suggestions when reading over parts of my first draft especial thanks must be given to Andrew Forrester, John Gardner, Jack Gray, John Harding and Radha Sinha. Their efforts have helped me improve what follows. Finally, thanks are due to my wife and family who have patiently put up with my neglect.

A.W.

Note on Spelling

With the exception of well-known geographical place names, the Chinese words in this book are spelt in accordance with the system devised by the Chinese in 1958 and used in Peking today. This system is known as *pinyin* and a full description of it can be found in most modern Chinese language textbooks. Since most readers will not be interested in a long linguistic description, the following list indicates the pronunciation of those letters which are very different from the sounds they represent in English spelling.

$$c = ts$$
$$q = ch$$
$$x = sh$$
$$z = dz$$
$$zh = j$$

Some familiar names which are transformed are Mao Tse-tung, which becomes Mao Ze-dong, and Chou En-lai, which becomes Zhou En-lai.

I

The Chinese World

The keynote of life in China today is change. One of the first things to strike a visitor to the country is the sense of purpose of the people, the feeling of a society on the move. Despite the many problems the country faces, there is an air of excitement and optimism. Each day seems to bring something new. Economic growth and technical modernisation are gradually transforming the environment, creating new jobs and bringing new material benefits. The spread of education, medical services and welfare organisations is improving the quality of life and raising expectations. As each change takes place the contrast with the old ways is plainly seen. At the same time there is a conscious drive to rebuild social morality, customs and institutions. China's citizens are surrounded by many challenges to their old cultural traditions. Since the process of change and growth is a slow one, the old and the new exist alongside each other constantly reminding everyone of how much remains to be done and what has already been achieved. In a factory traditional handicraft techniques are used beside sophisticated modern machines. In a village the bound feet and superstitions of the old women contrast with the active social roled played by their emancipated granddaughters.

China's immense population—now well over 800 million—and the vast size of the country add a further dimension to these contrasts. Each geographical region differs markedly from its neighbour. Daily work, food, clothing, housing and local customs are very different in the warm, moist rice-growing areas around Canton from the dry, dusty hills of the northwest or the forest-covered mountains of the northeast. A visitor travelling by train across the country immediately notices how each area has differ-

ent problems and is changing at a different rate. Such regional diversity adds to the difficulties facing the planners of economic and social development. Despite the unifying impact of the communist political system, everyday life is far from conforming to a simple uniform pattern.

The Old and the Young

Many of the contrasts in Chinese society reflect the differences between generations. While the Communist Party works to build a new morality, old traditions and methods linger on among those brought up before 1949. This not only influences minor things such as the way a house should be decorated or the design of clothes but also affects more important matters such as how marriages should be arranged, how children should be brought up, the role of women and the rules for social conduct. Throughout my visits to China, I have been struck by the vigour of many old customs. While the Communist Party finds strength in some of them such as the thrift and diligence of the peasants, it is also continually on its guard lest old cultural values should persist among the young and hinder the growth of the new society. As a result the young are gradually abandoning the ways of the past. Often this contrast between generations is matched by a contrast between areas. Remote parts of the countryside preserve traditional attitudes and change more slowly than modern cities like Shanghai.

The following passage is taken from a book called *Destroy Old Customs, Establish New Ways* published in 1965. It is typical of the large number of articles written in China aimed at overthrowing outmoded and potentially disruptive traditions.

Should parents ask for a 'Betrothal Gift' from their daughter's suitor?

Recently a moving story has been circulating in Shuang-wang Commune, Weinan Country, Shensi Province. It tells of the marriage of Liu Cong-fang, daughter of the famous model peasant Liu Shu-xian, to Li Hong-jin, a soldier and member of the Communist Youth League. When the marriage took place, Liu Shu-xian did not ask for a betrothal gift nor an elaborate ceremony and he only gave the couple a hoe and a shovel as presents. On the day of her marriage Liu Cong-fang rode a borrowed bicycle to the Li home accompanied by her sisters. The masses welcomed this model example of a new form of wedding.

Thus Liu Shu-xian and his daughter abandoned the old marriage customs. They set up a new style of thrift, economy and love of productive labour. They are truly praiseworthy. Their attitude has educational significance for parents and for young couples not yet married. Sometimes you still hear people in cities, towns and villages saying things like: 'whoever heard of not asking for a betrothal gift? It's always been the custom.' They consider new style marriages improper and even obey the old rules on giving and requesting gifts.

What should be our attitude towards such things? First we must clearly understand the nature of betrothal gifts. They are also known as 'body gifts' and 'contract gifts' and are the creation of the system of private ownership. They only came into being with class society and did not exist in ancient times. When the private ownership of wealth began and men seized authority lowering the status of women, betrothal gifts were introduced. As class society grew, women became the slaves of men, chattels to be bought and sold. Betrothal gifts were simply a way of setting a price for the body of a woman.

Such demands turn women into commodities. They reflect the superior status of men in the old society and the traditional marriage-by-purchase arranged by parents. They represent a system which insulted women and subjected them to great suffering. Therefore marriage-by-purchase was completely banned after Liberation.

Some people say that they know betrothal gifts are wrong but they need the money for their old age. In the old society it was true that the old had no social benefits. Once married a daughter could provide no support for her own parents. However, in today's socialist society things are quite different. The collective economy guarantees the material welfare of the old and the new Marriage Law calls upon married couples to care for both sets of parents rather than those of the man alone. We must patiently explain these changes to the old folk who suffered in the past.

In fact it is not only the old who are influenced by tradition.

2 *A study group considers the 'Communist Manifesto'*

Sometimes young girls also ask for betrothal gifts as an expression of their suitor's feelings. This not only shows that they love wealth more than the man but also that they preserve the old attitude of relying on the man for their livelihood. True love cannot be bought. It must be based on equality, mutual love and shared political principles. The man and woman are comrades as well as husband and wife.

Betrothal gifts are not simply a family matter. They are also related to the problem of complete liberation of women. Old social customs and the ideological remnants of the exploiting classes must be destroyed in order to build socialism. The complete liberation of women can only be achieved on the basis of economic, political and cultural equality with men. Betrothal gifts are an obstacle to this. Until women are free, their full productive powers cannot be liberated and social production will suffer.

In our transitional society today, classes and class struggle still exist. The overthrown exploiting classes are trying in all ways to sabotage socialism. They will use such old-fashioned things as betrothal gifts to spread bourgeois ideas about private ownership and self-indulgence and to corrupt people's revolutionary will. We must stand firm and deal with this matter seriously. We must resolutely abandon customs related to the old system and educate people who preserve such ways of thinking.

Writings like these are part of a continual social pressure for change throughout Chinese society. They show how seriously all aspects of life are discussed in relation to the Communist Party's ideals. While this drive to abandon old customs might appear rather excessive to outsiders, most Chinese I have met feel that efforts should be made to help modernise society. Nevertheless it is a source of conflict in people's behaviour and old habits die hard. Despite the propaganda efforts since 1949, the *People's Daily*, China's leading newspaper, still finds it necessary regularly to publish articles like the one above.

While attempting to transform the attitudes of the old, the Communist Party makes every effort to ensure that the younger generation is brought up with a very different outlook on the world. At work, in school and in their leisure time, they are taught to put the interests of the state and the collective above their own

3 *The* People's Daily, *8 March 1974. The editorial for International Women's Day calls on women to involve themselves in political struggle. Supporting articles give examples of what they can do.*

personal wishes. Those who are ambitious know that they have to conform to the new standards in order to get ahead. At the same time most young people are aware that radical changes are necessary to guarantee China's development. The students whom I taught in 1965 needed little encouragement to criticise Confucian traditions and the old superstitions of the past.

Nevertheless, during their childhood and as they read the old literature of China, the young inevitably absorb some traditional values. Family relationships still place emphasis on respect for the old and for one's parents. Old-fashioned courtesies are retained in social behaviour. Young people rarely arrange dates directly. Instead they prefer to ask someone else to act as an intermediary so that if the answer is no there are no unpleasant feelings or loss of face. Even during the Cultural Revolution of 1966 to 1969 when the Red Guards were called upon to become the vanguard of change and sweep aside the old culture, they were still hampered by the forces of tradition. One Shanghai newspaper pointed out:

Over thousands of years our family relations have been that the son obeys what his father says and the wife obeys what her husband says. Now we must rebel against this idea. . . . It should

18

no longer be a matter of who is supposed to speak and who is supposed to obey in a family but a matter of whose words are in line with Mao Ze-dong's thoughts. . . . If a grandfather's words are not in line with Mao Ze-dong's thoughts, it is absolutely justified for his grandson to rebel against him.

Public discussion of the need to change the values of the young continues today. Usually the problem is expressed in political terms as a struggle between the bourgeoisie and the proletariat for the political loyalty of China's youth. In this way cultural and social change at a basic individual level is related to the overall revolutionary goals of the Communist Party.

The developments of the past 25 years have broken down the environment in which the beliefs, attitudes and customs of the past had their roots. At the same time the persistence of the old has been a constraint on the speed and direction of further social change. The Cultural Revolution focused the attention of all Chinese on this problem when it called upon them to be 'critics of the old world'. When drawing up its policies, the Communist Party must always take this conflict between the old and the new into account. It is a conflict which underlines much of what happens in China today.

Methods of Change

The Communist Party employs a wide variety of methods to transform society. The most formal of these is the drafting of new laws to provide a legal framework for change. The Marriage Law of 1950 introduced the freedom of divorce, defined the rights and duties of children and gave equal status to women. It undermined the foundations of the traditional, male-dominated, authoritarian family and gave women a new world of opportunity. Other changes in the laws concerning ownership, employment, crime and so forth have in the same way altered the basis of economic and social relationships. Individuals cannot accumulate large amounts of wealth and it is more difficult for people in authority to grant favours to relatives and friends.

At the same time the new economic and social organisations have also forced change. Factory employment based on centralised planning, technical skills and standard wages have created a more impersonal relationship between employer and employee than the traditional ties of kinship and loyalty. It has also contributed to female emancipation by providing women with independent sources of income. The provision of education, medicine and welfare services by the state has swept aside the former reliance on family and friends for these things. In the countryside the disappearance of individual ownership of land and the stress on collective farming have had a similar effect. However, the fact that the nature of daily work in rural areas is much the same as it always was and that large groups of related people live near each other in villages has meant that the process has not been so obvious as in the cities.

The Communist Party also carries out straightforward political debate on the need to abandon old traditions. Often this is done through the system of study groups organised in all institutions. Every day either before work or during rest periods small groups of people come together under the guidance of Party members to read political essays and to relate the themes involved to their daily lives. According to some reports, such groups can easily become superficial with people saying what is expected of them and not bothering to think deeply about it. But during a large-scale political movement like the Cultural Revolution, they assume much greater importance. They meet more frequently and the discussions have a greater urgency. Everyone is aware that if he

4 *Wall posters during the Cultural Revolution. The slogan proclaims 'Defend Chairman Mao with blood and life'*

doesn't show a more positive attitude he might be open to criticism.

Apart from writings by Mao Ze-dong, most of the writings the groups study are newspaper reports and essays like the one above on marriage. The press in China is chiefly a medium for education and propaganda. Current events are reported but the aim is not simply to inform. Most reports serve as examples of the correct way to deal with a problem or are a means of drawing attention to a new policy. The newspaper report is interpreted by the study groups in the light of local conditions. A change in the content and terminology of newspapers acts as an important signal to the study groups about what they should be doing. A report describing how a factory economized on its use of raw materials, for example, encourages groups throughout the country to consider ways in which they too could save resources.

There are also a number of more formal organizations which permeate society and provide alternative ways of transmitting and debating new ideas. Apart from the Communist Party and the Communist Youth League, these include the trade unions, the women's associations, the 'little red guards' for the very young, and the militia. All of them are controlled by the Communist Party and are used to explain Party policy to outsiders and to report back on criticisms and problems. Since it is a tradition

5 *Workers demonstrate in Sian during the Cultural Revolution*

within the Communist Party to stress listening to the opinions of ordinary citizens and to encourage debate and criticism, these organisations are an important means of sounding out public opinion. Nevertheless, decisions are still ultimately taken by those in authority and the mass organisations are also a means of persuading people to conform to the political line of the Party.

Large-scale political campaigns intensify the political pressures on the individual and they are another important method of initiating change. The Communist Party has launched many of them since 1949. Sometimes they embrace a wide range of aims. The Cultural Revolution combined cultural and social change with an examination of governmental policies and a major struggle for power. At other times campaigns are more specific. The 'five anti' campaign of 1952 was directed at capitalists accused of the five abuses of bribery, tax evasion, theft of state property, cheating on government contracts and stealing national secrets. Political movements like these extend far beyond study groups. They involve street demonstrations, public rallies and denunciation meetings. As they unfold, individuals who are subject to criticism are under strong pressure to conform to the demands made on them. Should they actually be arrested, they are sent to carry out 'thought reform' through a period of physical labour combined with large amounts of political study. In its most intense form this entails a deep and painful reappraisal by the individual of his life and basic beliefs. Those who have experienced this process are unlikely to forget it.

Finally the most characteristic method of promoting cultural change in China is the use of model institutions and model individuals. The Communist Party almost always introduces its new policies and goals by putting forward examples for others to copy. One of the most famous of these is Dazhai Commune. Since 1964 all Chinese peasants have been called upon to copy and learn from the spirit of Dazhai. Each new development in agricultural policy is heralded by a report describing how it is implemented there. Thus in 1972 stories about Dazhai's investment in machinery underlined the renewed national emphasis on agricultural mechanisation. Other models are only used at a local level. In a cotton growing region a successful commune will be publicised so as to encourage its neighbours to copy its techniques.

Model people are also promoted in different ways. Some are

6 *'Battleground in the palm trees'; rural propaganda from the* People's Daily *combining many themes. To the left spring ploughing and mechanization. In the foreground the peasants denounce Lin Biao and soldiers arrive to help with the harvest*

prominent for a relatively short period of time or within a limited field. While their virtues are made clear, they are not built up into figures of heroic proportions. Wang Guo-fan is a peasant who was given great publicity in 1955 and 1956 for his work in setting up a cooperative farm. Sometimes he is still mentioned in the press but chiefly in the context of agricultural development. Model people who serve as examples of more general virtues are given much wider and continuous acclamation. Usually they are only given this status after their death and a common feature is the publication of a diary in which they have recorded their deeds and thoughts. Once a model is launched, plays, films, stories, poems and all the media are enlisted to drive the lessons home to the ordinary citizen. The model's original identity is rapidly surrounded by considerable idealisation.

The most famous of these models is the soldier, Lei Feng, who was first heard of in 1962. By 1965 my students knew all the details of his life. His example is that of an ordinary man dedicated to the Chinese Communist Party who did everyday work selflessly and to the best of his ability. His virtues are those that China's leaders would like to see widely adopted by all Chinese. Lei Feng died in a road accident in 1962. The following extract is typical of the hero and of the writings about him.

23

7 *Street propaganda on a large scale. A poster celebrating the centenary of the Paris Commune*

Lei Feng was born in a poor peasant family, and in his childhood he knew all the hunger, poverty, cruelty and degradation of the old society. Only after liberation was he able to eat regularly and go to school with books under his arm. Before joining the army in 1960, he worked as a tractor driver on a county-run state farm, and then in the Anshan Iron and Steel Company in northeast China. His deeds and the thick notebooks of his diary, totalling some 200,000 words, show his single-minded devotion to the noble ideal of working for the happiness of mankind and his constant concern with the problem of how to speed the building of socialism. Selfless and anxious to help others, he led a simple life and studied perseveringly. Full of youthful vigour he was diligent and modest.

8 January 1960 was Lei Feng's first day in the army. He bought a new diary for the occasion. On the first page he stuck a picture of Huang Ji-guang, the national hero who lost his life in the Korean war. Lei Feng looked at this picture every day and never ceased trying to measure up to his ideal.

Training of the new recruits began. Given a hand grenade, Lei Feng found he could not throw it the required distance, however hard he tried. He was very worried. When he was writing in his diary after supper that night, his eyes fell on the picture of Huang Ji-guang. He picked up the practice grenade, went to the drill ground, stationed himself facing the north wind, and threw it again and again. He was still at it when the squad leader found him long after the Lights Out bugle had sounded. His whole body ached so much after his efforts that he couldn't sleep. But he reminded himself in his diary, 'Think how you were tortured by scabies when you were a boy! Now you are training in order to be able to defend your homeland.

Why should a little pain bother you?'

Lei Feng became so absorbed with his studies that he often sat up until after midnight. He bought a flashlight so that he could read under the quilt when everyone else was asleep. 'After studying Chairman Mao's writings,' he wrote, 'I begin to understand how and for what to live. . . .' As his awareness deepened he set down thoughts such as: 'Two-thirds of the poor in the world are not yet liberated. Oppressed and exploited, they are underfed and lacking in clothes. I cannot look on while they are mistreated.'

Lei Feng held rigidly to a simple life. Except for what he spent for haircuts and the purchase of soap and some books, he banked all of his monthly allowance. He sewed cotton patches on his socks until there was practically nothing of the originals to be seen, and his wash basin and cup were covered with spots where the enamel had chipped off.

But Lei Feng was always ready to give help where help was needed. While he was stationed in Fushun, he saw people beating gongs and drums in the streets to announce the formation of a people's commune. Immediately he rushed to the bank, withdrew the 200 *yuan* that he had in his account and took it to the commune office. He wanted to contribute it to the reserve fund, he explained. When the commune leaders refused

8 *Lei Feng repairs his comrades' clothes while they sleep. An illustration from a children's comic book*

83 一天晚上，雷锋执行完任务回来，发现韩玉臣的裤子破了，他怕韩玉臣出操冷，就撕下自己的帽里子，一针一针地给补好。

25

to accept the money and suggested he send it home, he said, 'Home? This is my home. Except for the people I have nothing. The people have given me everything. Let this money play its part for the benefit of the people!' Moved by his earnestness and sincerity, the commune finally accepted half the sum. He took back the 100 *yuan* balance but when he read there was a serious flood around the town of Liaoyang, he sent it to aid the people who had suffered in the disaster.

For such actions, and because he refused to spend a penny on himself, some people called Lei Feng 'a fool'. On this he wrote in his diary, 'those who say I am a fool are wrong. My only desire is to be useful to the people and the country. If that is being a fool, I am glad to be one, for the revolution needs such fools, and so does the construction of our motherland.'

The Politics of Change

While the process of modernisation is gradually transforming the everyday life of the Chinese, the political debates within the Communist Party have added a further dimension of change and uncertainty. Despite the communists' firm conviction that their historical role is to build a communist society, they still have many disagreements over what methods to adopt and what the future should be like. At the same time the continual need to deal with urgent practical problems as they arise not only forces modifications to existing policies but also creates issues which divide the country's leaders. Problems of economic development, for example, involve both complex technical arguments and more far-reaching considerations of social organisation. Should industry or agriculture have priority? How should capital be invested? What is the best form of farm and factory organisation? What incentives should be used to make people work harder? As the following chapters show, there have been many changes of policy and sharp struggles between different groups within the Party who favour different answers. The apparent unity of ideology has not prevented political debates and conflict.

A fundamental reason for this can be found in the origins and development of the Communist Party itself. From the beginning it was clear that a successful revolution required both firm leadership and active participation by large numbers of ordinary people.

9 *Reading 'Quotations from Mao Ze-dang' at a demonstration. The quotations summarize some of the key elements in Mao's thinking*

While all Chinese communists accepted that this was so, there has been a constant tension between those who like to see completely centralised Party control and those who prefer more initiative from below. The former stress obedience and loyalty while the latter call for flexibility and debate at the grass roots level. In practice the Party has attempted to resolve this contradiction through the principle of 'democratic centralism'. This states that there should be scope for free discussion during the process of making a decision but once it is taken complete obedience to central orders is necessary. Nevertheless, the balance between the two poles is not clearly defined. At various times since 1949 the emphasis has shifted from one to the other. Mao Ze-dong, who believes that struggle between opposing views is a positive force in social development, welcomes the challenge of such shifts. Others have tended to seek a more gradual process of change.

The standpoint taken on this issue by different leaders within the Communist Party has shown itself in the type of development policies they have preferred. Those like Mao, who lean towards the 'democratic' pole, have stressed the use of policies first tried in the guerilla base area of Yenan before 1949. Wherever possible they stress greater decentralisation and the mobilisation of initiative from below. They rely on political education and inspiration to maintain discipline. Their style of leadership, called the 'mass line' by Mao, gives first place to building close relations with the masses, holding public discussions and accepting criticisms from subordinates. People in authority are expected to get out of their offices to investigate and gain practical experience before making decisions. They are criticized if they remain behind closed doors issuing commands. It was this approach that inspired the economic decentralisation of the Great Leap Forward in 1958 and led to the widespread freedom for ordinary people to criticize Party authorities during the Cultural Revolution.

By contrast others like Gao Gang in 1954, Peng De-huai in 1959 and Liu Shao-qi in 1966 have challenged Mao's policies. They have looked towards the Soviet Union for the ideas and methods to answer China's problems. Their approach emphasised gradual development through technical progress and central control and planning. They relied more on professional expertise than political mobilisation and tended to create large bureaucracies. Their style of leadership was characterised by comprehensive regulations and strong discipline. The opinions of the ordinary man were relatively neglected. The period of the First Five-Year Plan in the mid-1950's and of economic reorganisation in the early 1960's were both influenced by these trends.

However, these two approaches to political leadership in China have not always been in conflict. Indeed Mao and his opponents have at different times and over different issues shared many of the other's ideas. It was not until the Cultural Revolution that there was a full-scale confrontation. Using the 'mass line', Mao stepped outside the Communist Party and called upon the people, particularly the young Red Guards, to criticize his opponents' policies. The enthusiastic response he provoked showed that the ordinary person welcomed the chance to air his grievances. After an initial period of uncertainty, my students were soon willing to join in the debate. They were confident that by taking part in political debate they were speeding up the modernisation of their country. In fact the struggles of the Cultural Revolution were not so simple and led to considerable disorder in which many people lost sight of their early ideals. Eventually after a return to greater discipline, Mao succeeded in displacing Liu Shao-qi and his

10 *Cultural Revolution posters in Peking satirize Liu Shao-qi's policies*

associates.

For the man in the street changes like these have an important effect on his relations with political and governmental authorities. When the emphasis is on 'centralism', he faces a fairly predictable system of rules and regulations. Provided he obeys them and works well, he is likely to be rewarded by promotion or better pay. It is not so important for him to take part in political activities. When more attention is given to the 'mass line', the reverse is true. Political enthusiasm becomes more important than just doing a good job and following the rules. Strict discipline tends to break down and opportunity for promotion is given to those who show the sharpest political acumen. In this way political conflict within the Communist Party has a strong influence on the way people eager for social advancement behave as well as changing the relationship between leaders and led.

2
The Social Framework

Chinese society is dominated by three interlocking institutions, the Communist Party, the State Council and the People's Liberation Army. The Party gives the country political leadership. It sees itself as the guardian of the principles and values of the communist revolution. The State Council carries out the routine tasks of government. Its ministries and their subordinate organisations at provincial level and below manage the economy and implement the policies put forward by the Party. The Army serves both the political aims of the Party and the defence needs of the state. All three institutions thus have distinct social roles to play, with independent structures and chains of command.

However, the Communist Party is by far the most important and it has ultimate authority over the other two under the principle that the Party 'exercises overall leadership' of industry, agriculture, commerce, culture and education, the Army and the government. Whenever there has been a clash of interests, the Party has always been able to assert its control. Furthermore, Party members occupy all the key positions in the government, the Army and throughout society. This is especially true of the central leadership where major decisions are taken. In early 1974, Zhou En-lai was both a vice-chairman of the Party and Premier of the State Council, Ye Jian-ying was a member of the Party's political bureau (see below) and acting commander of the Army, and military leaders who were Party members were also active in government ministries. This interchangeability of personnel means that policies decided within the Party can be effectively carried out. Even at low levels within communes and factories, Party members usually do the most important jobs.

Although this close relationship makes it difficult in practice to distinguish between a man's role as an administrator and his role as a Party member, there is an important distinction to be made. As an administrator he has a specific job to do whether it is running a ministry or managing a factory. As a Party member he unites with others on the basis of shared values and beliefs. The Party provides him with the moral and political guidance which underlies all his other work. His aim is not simply to do a job but to promote and defend the communist view of the world. The Party maintains its organizational independence because it does not see itself as the government but as the mediator between the revolutionary aims of the people and the state structure set up to achieve those aims. Its members are expected to place communist values and the will of the revolutionary masses above any other loyalties.

The Role of the National Leadership

To most people outside China, the country appears dominated by a small group of national leaders. Mao Ze-dong, Chairman of the Communist Party and its ideological leader, stands prominently in the fore round. Premier Zhou En-lai, a vice-chairman of the Party, stands beside him efficiently managing the government. Other Party and government leaders like Deng Xiao-ping, Kang Sheng, Zhu De, Li Xian-nian and so forth continually appear in

11 *Mao Ze-dang, Zhou En-lai and Lin Biao at the opera in 1967*

a variety of roles. Until their disgrace in 1966 and 1971 respectively, Liu Shao-qi, the former Head of State, and Lin Biao, the then vice-chairman of the Party and commander of the Army, also belonged to this group. Most of these people have been leading figures in the Communist Party since the 1920s and 1930s. They shaped its rise to power and have directed the reconstruction of the country. They have not only successfully led a revolution and driven out foreign invaders, but have also presided over the first stages of a thorough-going social transformation. Between them they share all the qualities of a successful leadership, and it is not surprising to find the Chinese regarding them with the respect and deference that only great wartime leaders usually receive.

Mao Ze-dong's special position in this group is due not only to his organisational role as Chairman but also to his political and ideological guidance of the Communist Party. Since he became

12 *Mao's image is always present*

the effective leader of the Party in 1935, he has dominated practical decision making and overcome all resistence to his policies. He has also formulated and summed up in his writings the beliefs and methods of working which stand at the core of Party activity. He has not hesitated to ruthlessly discard opponents, and he has purposely built up his image as a great national leader to ensure the dominance of his ideas and of a Communist Party that follows his political line. Mao's picture can be seen throughout the country and his writings are read and publicized everywhere. The respect he gets reflects both his achievement in freeing and uniting the country, and the reality of his political power.

Although the political life of China has been directed by this small group of men in key positions, they have not always agreed amongst themselves on the policies to be adopted. The fragmentary reports available suggest that when they meet together, they hold frank and vigorous discussions, debating freely before they make decisions. Speeches by Mao Ze-dong informally reported by the Red Guards during the Cultural Revolution show a great deal of cut-and-thrust and an ability to be self-critical or to apologise. Sometimes these debates have eventually produced an agreed consensus. At other times, individuals have become centres of deep divisions which have led to splits within the Communist Party and struggles like those of the Cultural Revolution. In such cases questions of ideology have been complicated by the personal relationships and loyalties between various national leaders and their associates.

However, for the ordinary man the national leadership is remote and unapproachable. For him political and governmental power is realised through the local officials with whom he deals. As individuals, these officials react in a variety of ways to the ideological and practical pressures upon them, yet the central leadership has to rely on them to put into practice its values and policies. Therefore, the education and guidance of a body of reliable leaders, called cadres, is one of the major tasks of the Communist Party and a fundamental concern of key figures like Mao Ze-dong and Zhou En-lai.

The Cadre

A 'cadre' is someone with formal leadership power within an organisation. There are Party cadres, government cadres, military cadres and so forth. Most, though not all of them, are Party members and those that aren't are expected to come up to the same standards. In everyday use, the term is often extended to refer loosely to an official of any kind who by virtue of his work has some authority over the ordinary citizen. Since cadres are involved in making decisions and issuing orders, their attitudes and work-styles determine the character of Chinese society and how people feel about new policies.

The Party stresses that cadres must be politically correct as well as efficient at their jobs. They must provide moral leadership by setting an example and not turn into bureaucrats relying on red tape and rules and regulations. In theory they should be 'red and expert', which means combining professional efficiency with a drive to build communism, and they should follow Mao's 'mass line' style of leadership, which means personally discussing ideas with subordinates, accepting criticisms and suggestions, and patiently explaining new orders. They should not allow any barriers of privilege and authority to get in the way. In practice many cadres have not always lived up to these ideas. They are influenced by a bureaucratic tradition based on strict authority and a strong sense of social status. Many of them tend to feel a loss of face if they are criticised or their orders are questioned. At the same time there can be a conflict between administrative methods and political goals. The factory manager who pays bonuses to get a job done quickly may solve a production problem but by appealing to acquisitive instincts he undercuts the call for individuals to work selflessly for society in the same way as Lei Feng. During the Cultural Revolution many cadres were criticised for taking administrative shortcuts, neglecting political ideals, and turning into old-fashioned bureaucrats. Until 1966 the Party secretary at the language institute where I taught was held in considerable awe by the ordinary members of staff and he insisted on taking his meals in a private dining room. His superior attitudes were subsequently heavily criticised by the Red Guards as examples of political backsliding.

In the past the Party relied chiefly on special training to maintain the quality of cadres. There were exclusive cadre schools teaching ideology and methods and the Party issued specific propaganda and directives. In addition there was a drive to get cadres to take part in productive labour though the rules about this were never strictly enforced. Since the Cultural Revolution, political study and practical work have become a much more formal part of cadre life, particularly at middle and junior levels. Apart from regular weekly bouts of ordinary work alongside subordinates, all cadres now have to attend the new '7 May' cadre schools. These are named after the day in 1966 when Mao called upon all Chinese to combine theory and practice and to put politics first.

All cadres have to go to these schools at regular intervals for periods of several months or more. While there they do farming, small-scale industrial work and study political writings. Large institutions like Peking University run their own cadre schools. Others are run by city districts and take people such as medical officers, traffic controllers and teachers from small schools. The leaders of the cadre school serving Chong-wen District in Peking, which I visited in 1971, told me that they believed this regular physical work would ensure that cadres do not forget their political values and would give them a closer understanding of the life of ordinary people. They also thought that these schools would become a long-term feature of Chinese society in order to prevent cadres forming a new ruling class. They certainly did not see the schools as punishment for cadres who had made mistakes. Whether their hopes will be realised remains a moot point. Certainly in early 1974 the Chinese media still carried occasional complaints

13 *An accountant and a law court official learn to be blacksmiths at the Chong-wen cadre school*

about cadres being authoritarian or using their rank to obtain special privileges. On the other hand most visitors to China agree that the relationship between cadres and ordinary people has relaxed since the Cultural Revolution with much greater willingness to exchange opinions and accept criticism.

At the cadre schools life is well-organised and demanding. The cadres live in dormitories and have a fixed daily routine. The aim is to make all schools self-supporting. At the Chong-wen school, the cadres grew rice and vegetables, raised pigs, chickens and geese, and had small carpentry and blacksmith's workshops. The daily timetable in 1971 was a follows:

0620	Reveille and physical exercises.
0700	Daily study of the writings of Mao Ze-dong.
0800	Breakfast.
0830	Work, either in the fields or the workshops.
1200	Lunch followed by a rest.
1400	Work.
1800	Dinner.
1900	Newspaper study.
1930	Political meetings, study, or private time.
2200	Lights out.

In most cases a cadre's family stays at home and, if necessary, a cadre can take a few days leave to deal with family matters.

A major factor governing a cadre's career is his personal file. This is kept within his work unit and records all the important facts about his life including such things as his family and class origins, his technical qualifications, the quality of his work and his attitudes towards various political issues. When a cadre is considered for promotion, this file forms the basis for judgement. Naturally, everyone works hard to avoid getting a black mark on his record. During the Cultural Revolution these files became the centre of considerable debate. Political opponents used them to attack each other and the Red Guards were able to get a lot of confidential information from them about cadres. Several of the most intense local struggles concerned whether a cadre had been correctly labelled during the course of the movement or whether an earlier judgement should be reversed. Since 1969, public discussion of the role of personal files has ceased and it may be that their importance is declining with the switch in emphasis to continuous cadre training in the '7 May' cadre schools.

14 *Chong-wen cadres doing political study*

One further aspect of the life of China's cadres that many visitors and scholars have noticed is that it is possible to distinguish between several generations. The oldest, who occupy the most senior positions, are those that joined the Communist Party during its first decade. Next come those that joined during the war against Japan and the subsequent war of liberation. Between them these two groups account for nearly all the key leadership posts in China. Cadres who joined the Party and government after 1949 did so in association with specific activities such as agrarian reform, economic planning and various political campaigns. While they have achieved a good deal of social mobility, moving upwards to better jobs, they have not yet displaced the veterans in the top positions. Although cadre training stresses comradeship and cooperation between these generations of cadres, there has at times been friction. After the Cultural Revolution old cadres who had been criticised found it very difficult to get on with new cadres promoted from among the Red Guards. The Party had to issue a lot of propaganda on this problem, praising the experience of the old and the vigour of the young. Thus the potential conflict between generations of cadres with different experience and origins is something that the Party leadership has to take into account.

The Communist Party

Since it was founded in 1921, the Chinese Communist Party has experienced many major organisational reforms. During the first 15 years of its life, it faced a desperate situation and was nearly destroyed by inner dissension and by attacks from its enemies. The advice it received from the Soviet Union only added to its troubles. It was not until after the Long March, in the relative security of the Yenan base area, that the Party developed a style and integrity of its own under Mao's leadership. Nevertheless, the new problems associated with the assumption of power after 1949 in turn led to further organisational change. At various times the Party has experimented with different types of regional sub-divisions and has altered its degree of control of other social bodies. The most recent large-scale changes along these lines came during the Cultural Revolution. At the Party's Ninth Congress in 1969, its constitution was revised to give greater organisational simplicity and its leading position in society was reaffirmed. It is likely that future congresses will make further changes.

The structure of the Party is strongly hierarchical. At present there are four organisational levels. They are (1) the central bodies, (2) the provinces, autonomous regions and major cities, (3) the counties and smaller cities, and (4) the basic levels in communes, factories etc. These divisions parallel the geographical divisions of government. At each level the Party committees are elected by a congress of delegates from subordinate Party units within the area and approved by the authorities at the level above. As well as electing the Party committees, the congresses also set out the guidelines for the committees' work during the coming period. However the responsibility for drafting the guidelines in fact rests with the committees. According to the Party's constitution, national congresses should be held every five years and provincial and county level congresses every three years but these meetings have not always been held on time and the delays have reflected divisions within the Party leadership. In the 25 years since 1949 there have only been three national congresses and the latest, the tenth since the Party was formed, was held in 1973.

At the central level, the national congress elects a central committee which in turn elects a Party chairman and a political bureau. This bureau, and particularly its standing committee which meets regularly, is the key leadership body in China. The chairman controls its meetings and it formulates all major policies. The central committee also establishes a number of departments and offices. Some of these are concerned with internal Party affairs such as administration, personnel and discipline. Others deal with external matters such as economic and military policies and foreign affairs. Until the Cultural Revolution, these departments were very important and were headed by a powerful general secretary. Since 1969 they have been reduced in number and the post of general secretary has disappeared.

The ordinary members of the central committee are drawn from all areas of Party life. Most provincial leaders are included as well as leading military and government figures. Their membership of the central committee reflects their importance to the Party and their right to be consulted in major political discussions. It does not mean that they have to participate in central committee work every day. In fact full meetings of the central committee, called plenums, are only held once or twice a year. In times of political division they are often delayed. No plenum was called between 1962 and 1966 when the issues that led up to the Cultural Revolution were being debated. In addition to these plenums, the political bureau can also call extraordinary or enlarged meetings of the central committee to deal with specific problems. In these cases not all central committee members need be present and outside personnel may be called in.

The organisation of Party committees at provincial and county levels parallels that of the central committee but it grows progressively simpler further down the hierarchy. Day-to-day business is carried out by a standing committee headed by a secretary and a group of deputies. At provincial level, these people run a number of bureaus which handle both internal Party affairs and external government policies. In the counties, the bureaus are smaller and the Party officials may do more than one job. At the lowest level in factories, communes, schools and so forth, there are either committees or branches. In large institutions the committees may have a secretary and several colleagues with branches under their control. In small ones the branches may only have a secretary with little formal organisation. Whenever a new enterprise is established, a Party unit is formed within it. Whenever a Party member moves to a new job, he is transferred to the Party unit at his new place of employment. Directives and information flow down through the hierarchical structure and requests and reports are passed back up. The independence of this organisation from the governmental and managerial work in which many members are involved has enabled the Party to react swiftly at critical moments and given it a boldness and drive to make radical changes where more cautious administrative bodies may have hesitated.

The chief source of income for the Party is the dues paid each year by its members. It also obtains some funds from its own enterprises such as publications and its magazine, *Red Flag*. This money is used to finance Party activities and to pay the salaries of full-time Party workers. However, since many Party cadres are paid by the unit they work for, the Party does not have to finance all its officials. In addition much of its propaganda work is carried out by other bodies such as the trade unions and the women's associations and many of its communications are carried through normal government channels.

Membership of the Party is open to 'any Chinese worker, poor peasant, lower-middle peasant, revolutionary armyman or any other revolutionary element who has reached the age of 18'. An applicant must be recommended by two Party members, fill out an application form and undergo a thorough scrutiny by the Party branch he seeks to join. He must be approved by the members of that branch and by the committee at a higher level. In practice people who aspire to become Party members must show their political activism over a long period. It is also usual for most of them to belong to organisations such as the Communist Youth League before joining the Party. Sometimes the Party has expanded quite rapidly such as after the Cultural Revolution when large numbers of young activists enrolled. At other times the process has slowed down such as during the mid-1950s when attempts were made to raise the quality of membership after the rapid expansion of the late 1940s. By 1973 there were 28 million members or roughly four people out of every hundred. From 60 to 70 per cent of them are peasants and around 10 per cent are women. For most of these people Party life consists of regular attendence at Party meetings to discuss ideological and practical problems and of active work to spread Party ideals and policies throughout society.

The Government

Despite the great changes that have taken place in the actual operation of government in China over the past 25 years, the formal structure (see the diagram on page 43) still remains similar to that laid down by the Constitution of the People's Republic adopted in 1954. In theory the source of all administrative authority is the National People's Congress which consists of delegates elected to represent the provinces, autonomous regions and directly-administered major cities. There are 22 provinces (including Taiwan), 5 autonomous regions and 3 directly-administered cities. The autonomous regions function in the same way as provinces except that concessions are made within them to the customs and languages of the non-Chinese national minorities which make up most of their population. According to the Constitution, the Congress should meet once a year and a new Congress should be elected every four years. When it is not in session, its work should be carried out by its standing committee. In practice, since it was set up in 1954, only three Congresses have been elected (in 1954, 1959 and 1964) and during their lifetime most of the work was done by the standing committees.

Until the Cultural Revolution, the National People's Congress had three main tasks, the appointment of the Chairman of the Republic with various special offices, the formulation of the laws to be administered by the judiciary and the approval of the work of the State Council which carries out the day-to-day business of government through its subordinate ministries. In 1966 this work came to a halt and the position of Chairman of the Repulic was unofficially abandoned. From 1969 onwards, China's leaders occasionally referred to the need to convene a new Congress and revise the Constitution but by 1974 no visible progress had been made. In effect, therefore, the government of China is administered by the State Council under the indirect control of the central leadership of the Communist Party. Whatever reforms are made by a new National People's Congress, this basic link between

Party and government will continue.

The State Council is headed by a Premier and a number of Vice-premiers. They control a variety of offices and ministries concerned with different aspects of government work. Until the mid-1950s there was a tendency for the number of ministries to grow and to assert direct control over their departments and agencies in the provinces. During the Great Leap Forward in 1958, this process was reversed. Ministerial power was reduced and control of provincial level activity was handed over to the provincial authorites. Subsequently a balance was struck between central and provincial control but during the Cultural Revolution there was further decentralisation of power and a great reduction in the number of ministries and offices. The main impact of this decentralisation has been to allow greater coordination of policy at provincial level. With the exception of a few strategic industrial, financial and commercial bodies, the ability of central ministries to work independently in the provinces is now very limited. Nevertheless, the problem of balancing centralised planning with local coordination and initiative is one that requires constant attention. In practice there is a good deal of variation between provinces and between ministries.

In the provinces, autonomous regions and major cities, the constitutional position was similar to that at the central level. Provincial People's Congresses oversaw the work of Provincial People's Committees which had subordinate bureaus corresponding to the State Council's ministries. However, as a result of the Cultural Revolution all these bodies have been swept aside and replaced by Provincial Revolutionary Committees. These emerged as a mixture of former provincial leaders, local military commanders, and representatives of the Red Guard organisations. They have been approved by the Party central committee and by the State Council and they are explicitly led by the Provincial Party Committees. They have representatives of the ordinary people on them and they have bureaus to carry out the actual government. In the counties and ordinary municipalities, the situation is very similar to that in the provinces. As the accompanying diagram shows, there are the same kind of formal and informal organizations and linkages.

Although there are some subordinate units of government beneath the county and municipal level, for most practical

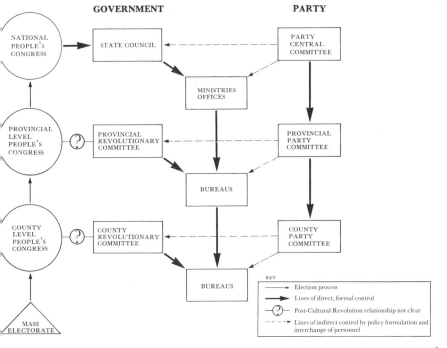

GOVERNMENT   PARTY

NATIONAL PEOPLE'S CONGRESS

STATE COUNCIL

PARTY CENTRAL COMMITTEE

MINISTRIES OFFICES

PROVINCIAL LEVEL PEOPLE'S CONGRESS

PROVINCIAL REVOLUTIONARY COMMITTEE

PROVINCIAL PARTY COMMITTEE

BUREAUS

COUNTY LEVEL PEOPLE'S CONGRESS

COUNTY REVOLUTIONARY COMMITTEE

COUNTY PARTY COMMITTEE

BUREAUS

MASS ELECTORATE

KEY

Election process
Lines of direct, formal control
Post-Cultural Revolution relationship not clear
Lines of indirect control by policy formulation and interchange of personnel

purposes Chinese society is thereafter divided directly into its working components—communes, factories, commercial enterprises, educational institutions and so forth. With the exception of the largest and most strategic of these which are operated at provincial level, these working units deal directly with the county and municipal authorities and not with any intervening bodies. While some scope is allowed for them to interact with each other independently, the government generally limits the extent to which this can be done outside of the national and local economic plans. Unofficial trading in raw materials and end products between enterprises is not allowed.

Much of the work of government consists of drawing up directives and circulars in response to policy initiatives from above or from the Party and to problems thrown up from below. Usually this involves investigation and the gathering of information, sometimes by extensive surveys of the units concerned. When central budget and development plans are drawn up, consultations are first held with provincial levels before directives are issued. This process is then repeated down through the system until the plans are implemented at the basic level.

The ordinary citizen has a variety of direct and indirect contacts with his government. If he is over 18, he can vote for

15 *Small arms drill for the PLA*

people previously approved by the Party to serve on the people's congresses. When dealing with the police, obtaining a licence, paying rent for publically owned housing and borrowing from a bank, he is also directly in touch with the lower branches of government. But for the most part, his contacts are formed indirectly through his employment. Ration coupons, medical and welfare arrangements, changes of job, long distance travel permits and so forth are all handled by his employers. As a result, the average Chinese citizen only has a limited direct experience of the formal governing bodies. His personal involvement in the running of his country is chiefly expressed through the mass campaigns and political organisations inspired and led by the Communist Party.

The People's Liberation Army

In contrast to most military forces throughout the world, the People's Liberation Army (PLA) has both a military and a social role to play. As an army it has a similar structure to others. There are a number of service arms including the air force, navy, infantry, artillery, and signals. These tend to function together in task forces rather than entirely separately. The chain of command is centralised and stretches down through divisions, regiments, battalions, companies and platoons. Although much of its equipment is old-fashioned, there is a supply of modern weapons ranging from small arms to atomic bombs and long-range

44

missiles. As a social force, the PLA is closely connected with political life. Its leaders are prominent both in the Communist Party and in the government. It runs a large number of economic units ranging from state-owned farms to transport services and large factories. Soldiers also spend a proportion of their time outside their barracks working in communes and factories either as ordinary labourers or as leaders. Through its leadership of the militia, the PLA's military influence is carried into most social units. In addition, the PLA acts as a pacesetter for the rest of society. Propaganda usually embodies it with all the political virtues that everyone should learn. This was especially true of the period before and during the Cultural Revolution when the PLA was one of the mainstays of the Maoist wing.

Overall command of the PLA is exercised by two related bodies, the Military Affairs Commission of the Party and the Ministry of National Defence of the State Council. In practice these share the same personnel. The day-to-day running is controlled by the PLA General Headquarters which consists of professional soldiers. Thus Mao's principle that 'the Party commands the gun, and the gun must never be allowed to command the Party' is strictly adhered to, even though the interrelationship between PLA and Party leadership is so close. Geographically the PLA is organised into 11 military regions which are in turn divided into provincial military districts. The field armies are stationed throughout the country with the largest concentrations opposite the island of Taiwan, still held by the Nationalists, and on the borders with the Soviet Union. The PLA has no overseas bases.

The internal organisation and life of the PLA reflects its political ideals and social roles. The officer system with special ranks and commissions was abolished in 1965. Thereafter soldiers leading units were simply referred to as commanders of the units concerned. Differences in uniforms were reduced to a minimum and the scale of salaries was made slightly more equal. Commanders also share in the barrack-room and social life of their men. Of the approximately 3 million soldiers in the PLA, only the commanders, technical experts and special units are regulars. The rest are conscripts doing from two to four years' service depending on which branch they join. Everyone over the age of 18 is liable to be drafted but only a percentage of the more mentally and physically able are taken. People deprived of their political rights are

16 *The 196th Division helps peasants from a nearby commune. Even the Divisional Commander (left foreground) makes a token effort*

not qualified to serve, and only sons may be exempted or deferred. When this system was introduced in 1954, there was some popular opposition but the prestige now accorded the PLA and the fact that military training also provides useful technical skills that can be employed after demobilisation have overcome this. Most young people today say that one of their ambitions is to become a soldier.

The key unit of army life is the company, which consists of around 100 men. Political and social activity is centred at this level. In the 196th Division which is stationed near Peking each company occupies a barrack block with commanders and men sharing dormitories. As well as a military commander, each company has a political instructor who concentrates on the political training of the men. This takes up 30 per cent of a soldier's time. Another 20 per cent is taken up by productive labour either in the Division's own fields and workshops or in communes outside. As a result of this the Division grows about 80 per cent of its own food and can supply the state with some of the vitamins and anti-biotics it produces in its pharmaceutical factory. The remaining 50 per cent of a soldier's time is taken up with military

17 *Good relations between the Army and the people is a constant theme. Leaving a village early in the morning, the water is drawn and food is left with a letter of thanks*

training.

The Party branch organizes the formal Party life of the company and oversees the work of the Revolutionary Fighters' Committee. This committee has 15 members, 5 of them are cadres the rest being ordinary soldiers. It takes charge of barrack life and also runs a company club for leisure time activities and for maintaining company morale by teaching its history and discussing contemporary world events. The Revolutionary Fighters' Committee has sub-committees for economic work, art and propaganda, mass work, and the posting of propaganda on the barrack walls. The participation of soldiers in the running of the company is a product of the democratic traditions of the PLA stretching back to its guerrilla days before 1949. Nevertheless, in actual military situations full authority is accorded to the commanders. Although commanders are on a higher salary scale, often receiving three or four times the average soldier's salary of 10 *yuan* (in March 1974 there were 4·60 *yuan* to the £1) per month, the general life style which stresses simplicity, thrift and industriousness is shared by all. As a result of this internal democracy and of the intense political education within the PLA, the impression the outsider receives is of an army with very high morale and a deep commitment to the social goals of the Communist Party. This impression is fostered by the great effort the PLA makes to build good relations with the people at large. The example of Lei Feng is taken as the model for all soldiers.

Apart from its economic assistance to communes and factories by actually helping in productive work, the PLA also contributes to the training of the people's militia. Militia units are organised by all institutions as part of China's defensive forces and also as an aid to internal security. Most able-bodied people take part and this involves regular drills and exercises. In most institutions the militia work is run by demobilised soldiers and they liaise with the PLA, getting extra military and political assistance when necessary.

During the Cultural Revolution, the political role of the PLA was considerably enhanced. When former Party and government leaders were criticized, their work was often taken over by military leaders. Although the attempted coup in 1971 by the former Commander-in-Chief, Lin Biao, raised the threat of a military takeover, it did not materialize and the PLA remained loyal to the Party. Thereafter there was a decline in the number of soldiers serving in the Party and government as more and more civilian leaders were promoted or rehabilitated. Nevertheless, the PLA remains a major force on the political scene. Its economic role as a builder of roads and railways and a mainspring of development in border regions is still vital. Furthermore, as a political paragon and as the trainer of technicians and political activists who, when demobilized carry their skills and beliefs out into society with them, the PLA is an important element in the social transformation of China.

3
Down to the Countryside

China is a land of peasants. Even in the largest city, you can see peasants selling their goods or buying supplies to take back home. Of the 800 million population, around 80 per cent live in the countryside earning their livelihood from the land. Their lives are governed by the demands of the agricultural calendar. In the past, their fight for social justice and an escape from grinding poverty contributed to the revolution that brought the Communist Party to power. Today the need to increase their productivity and raise their standard of living is at the heart of China's policies for economic development.

Since 1949, the Communist Party has brought about a fundamental reorganisation of the social and economic life of the peasants. The outcome has transformed both their relationships with each other and with the land. It has also undermined traditional peasant attitudes and values. In all his activities, from the way his work is organized to the way his family life is run, the peasant is faced with a conflict between new and old ways of doing things. This conflict affects much that happens in the countryside today and the agrarian reforms implemented by the Party have to take account of the tension it produces. Nevertheless, China's future depends on finding a successful solution to the problems of agricultural development.

A Land of Contrasts

China's peasants are not equally distributed across its 3.7 million square miles. In fact 95 per cent of the population live on only 40 per cent of the land. More than half of China consists of the arid steppeland and deserts of the northwest, and the high mountains

49

and plateaus of the west. With poor soils, little rain and great extremes of temperature, these vast regions barely support 5 per cent of the population. The remainder live in the valleys, plains and river deltas of the east and south where nearly all of China's cultivable land is found. This concentration of population in a limited area has created an extremely intensive system of agriculture. All resources are carefully organised to yield the optimum return and nothing is wasted. Wherever conditions permit, the peasants raise two and sometimes even three crops per year on the same piece of land.

Climate and topography have not only influenced the pattern of population distribution, they have also created many distinctly different agricultural regions. A major factor is the impact of the monsoon cycle. In winter, the high air pressure over central Asia causes cold, dry air to flow out towards the sea. North China experiences hard frosts and bitter northwest winds which sometimes raise heavy dust storms. Even areas as far south as Shanghai remain surprisingly cold. In summer, the situation is reversed. Warm, moist air is drawn across the land from the sea bringing rain with it. The further northwest it travels, the drier this air becomes until eventually over the deserts of Sinkiang and Inner Mongolia the rainfall ceases altogether. The importance of this annual cycle with its concentration of rain in the summer months is reflected in the environments of the different regions. The greatest differences are between the wheat growing areas of the north and the rice growing areas of the south but, even within these, there are variations in crops and growing seasons. Inevitably these environmental differences produce striking contrasts in the way of life of the people.

The northwestern province of Sinkiang receives the least of the monsoon rains. It consists of a series of desert basins surrounded by high mountains. Into the edges of these basins drain rivers fed by the glaciers and snows on the mountains. Since rainfall is negligible, all farming relies on this source of water, and crops of wheat, coarse grains and fruit are grown during the short summer. Housing is strongly built to withstand the extremes of temperature, ranging during the year from $-20°F$ to over $100°F$, and the people need both thick furs and light cotton clothes. Large areas of the province are used for grazing sheep, which are an important source of food and leather. However, the sparse vegetation restricts the size of the flocks and forces a nomadic life on the shepherds. The indigenous population are mainly Uighurs and Kazakhs, who are moslems of Turkish origin quite distinct from the Chinese—a fact which is shown in their language, food, and culture. Since 1949 large numbers of Chinese have gone to Sinkiang as part of government programmes to improve irrigation and control desert expansion. While economically and politically integrated with the rest of the country, Sinkiang remains very untypical of the Chinese way of life.

By contrast, the loess region which covers much of the north China provinces of Kansu, Shensi and Shansi has been continuously occupied and cultivated by the Chinese for many thousands of years. The loess is a fine yellowish-brown soil which has been blown by the winds from the northwestern deserts and deposited in layers often tens or hundreds of feet deep on top of the original terrain. It is exceptionally fine and easily eroded by wind and water, leaving the vertical earth cliffs and precipitous ravines and gullies so typical of the region's landscape. The silt that is carried away by the Yellow River forms the soil of the North China Plain to the east. With limited rainfall and a short growing season, the peasants have a hard struggle to raise their basic crops of wheat, millet, corn, kaoliang and cotton. Traditionally the winter was a slack season when little could be done and the peasants were idle. The spring and summer were periods of intense activity when all available labour was needed for ploughing, planting and harvesting, especially in areas growing two crops. The collectivisation of agriculture since 1949 has evened out the load with better mobilisation of labour for the busy seasons and land improvement work during the winter. Much greater effort is now put into carving the loess into terraced fields and building large-scale irrigation works.

Although modern industry is steadily supplying more goods to the countryside, the peasants still meet most of their needs themselves. Because the loess is easily worked, they build their homes by digging cave houses back into the hillsides. These are famous for their warmth in winter and coolness in summer. Local handicrafts produce most of the basic farm equipment such as the wicker baskets, stone rollers and wooden implements. The women weave their own cotton cloth for the black, padded clothes and shoes of winter and the thin clothes of summer. The favourite

18 *Terraces in the Loess hills of Dazhai*

staple food is wheat ground into flour and made into noodles or steamed buns. These are usually eaten with a dish of vegetables flavoured with chilli and garlic. Meat is expensive and at best eaten a few times a month. Pork is the most popular, as everywhere in China, but more mutton is consumed here than elsewhere in the country. The peasants from other parts of China look upon those from the loess as dour, hardworking and a little miserly. Characteristics that certainly match the harshness of a region which frequently has had to fight to overcome drought or other disasters. It is no surprise that the model commune of Dazhai, famous for its self-reliance and perseverance, is found here.

Further south, in the Yangtze Delta, life is much easier. The summers are longer, the rain more reliable, and the land fertile. Strewn across the flat plain are many lakes, ponds, rivers and canals, providing irrigation, drainage and easy communications. Nearly all of the land is double cropped with early harvests of barley, wheat, or beans followed by the major crop of rice. The working year of the peasants is much longer than in the north, though the problems of land management are less arduous. The ease of transport and strategic location have long made the Delta a key economic area. The presence of modern Shanghai has added to its importance and strengthened the commercial nature of the agriculture. Cotton, tea, silk and vegetables are all important crops. In addition pigs, chickens, ducks and fish are all widely raised. These, together with boiled rice or noodles, are the distinctive foods of an area which is famous for its rich sauces. The people have a reputation for grace and beauty which is reflected

19 *Canals grace the villages and towns of Yangtze Delta*

in the fine silk embroidered shoes, aprons and bonnets worn by the peasant women on special days, and by the elegant, white-washed houses with tile roofs which stand alongside the canals over which arch graceful bridges. They are also known for their gaiety and culture, which has created a wealth of local musical and artistic traditions. The northern Chinese tend to think of them as spendthrifts, rather frivolous and too clever by half. This feeling of difference is reinforced by the strong local dialects which are unintelligible to the speakers of the standard language of the north.

Yet another way of life is found in the hilly provinces south of the Yangtze, particularly in the subtropical province of Kwang-tung. Separated from the rest of the country by mountains, it has always maintained an air of independence once again strengthened by the distinctness of the local Cantonese dialect. The rugged landscape is a mixture of poor quality hill land and rich valleys and deltas. The scarcity of good land once led to a steady rate of emigration overseas. Many of the Chinese communities in other parts of the world originally came from this province. However, the hot climate, plentiful rain and all-year growing season brings rich harvests to the land that is farmed. Two crops of rice can easily be grown, as well as a wide variety of fruits and vegetables. The peasants are busy the whole year round, and maintenance of the paddy fields takes a great deal of effort. Because of the warm weather, winter clothes are not really needed and simple cotton clothes are enough for most occasions. When working in the

fields, most peasants wear little more than shorts and a straw hat. Their brick houses are designed to withstand the heavy rains and usually have wide eaves to provide extra shelter. Pigs are still a major source of meat though more fish and duck are eaten than elsewhere. The local preference is for sweet and delicate flavours and much of Chinese food eaten abroad is derived from the Cantonese style of cooking. To the rest of the population the Cantonese appear an excitable and emotional people, and not very reliable. They are thought of as 'uncivilized' but in turn regard the northerners as 'barbarians'.

The above descriptions give some idea of the diverse environments in which the Chinese live. Nevertheless, despite periods of internal unrest, the country has always maintained a political and cultural cohesion, united by its unified ideology and system of government and by the broadly similar patterns of peasant social organisation. Whatever the differences in everyday life, the reforms and methods of the Communist Party are much the same in all the regions.

The Rural Inheritance

On coming to power the Communist Party inherited a rural society shaped by three institutions: a system of small-scale private

55

landownership dominated by petty landlords, a widespread division into close-knit kinship groups, and a marketing structure which limited the social and economic horizons of the peasants to their own localities. In addition the effects of war and of corrupt Nationalist government had severely disrupted and exhausted the agricultural economy. By 1949 markets were stagnating, inflation was rampant and production was far below its pre-war levels. Most people were longing for strong, honest government. These were the foundations upon which the Party set out to build a new society.

In terms of landownership the Party divided the rural population into landlords, rich peasants, middle peasants, poor peasants and labourers. Landlords were defined as those who owned land but did not personally farm it. Instead their main source of income were land rent, interest from money lending, and industrial and commercial enterprises. Some landlords hired labourers to work some of their fields but the richer ones had become absentee landlords living in towns and cities. They collected their rents through middlemen who were often corrupt. The category of rich peasants included those who owned most of their land and farm implements and could afford to rent in more land for profitable commercial farming. Though they worked the fields themselves, they also hired some labourers. Occasionally they rented out land and did a little money-lending, but on a much smaller scale than landlords. Middle peasants owned part of their land and rented part. They had adequate tools and depended chiefly on their own labour. Poor peasants had few tools and insufficient land. They were forced to rent in land to survive and had to supplement their income by labouring for others for at least part of the year. Labourers were defined as those who depended entirely on the work they did for others.

While the Party attempted to define its categories precisely, in practice it was very difficult to find the boundaries between them. Communist sources usually state that the landlords and rich peasants made up less than 10 per cent of the rural population but owned 70 per cent of the land. This probably overestimates the degree of concentration of landownership. A sample survey carried out under the direction of J. L. Buck in 1929–33 suggested that they only held 46 per cent of the land. Nevertheless, there was a great deal of regional variation, with areas both better and worse than either of these estimates.

While the differences in the amount of land owned were not great, they were vital in terms of economic security and social status. The poor peasant had a constant fight to pay his rent and support his family on a farm often no bigger than one acre, dotted about the village in small plots rather than as one unit. In most cases rent was paid in kind and the landlords took either a fixed amount of grain or a share in the harvest. The lowest rate was around 40 per cent of the crop but it was often more and sometimes reached as high as 80 per cent. Payment in cash was less common and chiefly used where the crop was not grain.

The right to collect rent was not the only economic power the landlords had over their peasants. They also dominated local finance and credit facilities through commerce, pawnbroking and money-lending. Interest rates on loans were generally very high and many peasants found repayment a greater problem than rent. For many the path lay through debt and mortgage of their land to losing their land and becoming tenant farmers. The rich peasants and the bulk of the better off relied on the income from their larger landholdings to stave off this eventuality.

Kinship groupings were much stronger in south China than in the north but the ideas behind them were much the same everywhere. Each family saw itself together with many other related families of the same name as part of a lineage, sometimes called a 'clan', which traced its descent through the male line back to a common male ancestor. In the south they occasionally had many thousands of members divided into subgroups and occupying whole villages. More commonly a village was the home of two or three lineages of differing strengths. In the north there was much more fragmentation and most lineages amounted to little more than a loose grouping of a few related families.

Within a lineage each family had a great degree of economic independence and both rich and poor could be found. However, the larger unit brought them together in many ways. A well-run lineage kept records of its history and the relationships between its member families. It organized ceremonies to celebrate its common ancestry and the honour that the achievements of individual members reflected on the group as a whole. The council of elders settled internal disputes and organized cooperation by many families for large-scale projects such as land reclamation. Rich lineages owned land and buildings which were maintained for the good of all, though often these resources could be selfishly exploited by their more powerful families. The members of a lineage were expected to fulfil duties and obligations towards it but in return they shared the joint benefits and received its protection. Even in those areas where lineages were not strong, their spirit fired family life and governed the way large families expanded in times of wealth. Essentially the system depended on the relationship between old and young. Reverence for the common ancestor kept the group together and within a family this was translated into strict filial obedience and firm rules of precedence for the old over the young. Great care was taken to define the relationship and status of all the members of the family no matter how distant. Thus each person fitted into a prescribed order and behaved accordingly.

In terms of rural society as a whole, the lineage provided a base from which the individual could operate. He knew that he could fall back on it for support against outsiders. It was a central part of his life and he always thought of himself as a member of the larger group. This created strong loyalties which could cut across other economic and political relationships. The lineage was also independent of the formal government. It maintained internal discipline and settled disputes with other groups without recourse to the authorities. While economic and social changes in the towns had undermined this system by 1949, its hold on the countryside remained strong. Even now it has not entirely disappeared. During the Cultural Revolution, reports in the press complained that 'clan' loyalties and disputes were still conflicting with the new political ideals.

Kinship groupings contributed to the strong attachment of the peasants to their localities, which centred on a market all the people of the area could conveniently use. The peasants carried out all their buying, selling and other business within these localities through a network of trusted friends, relatives and contacts. Since commercial practice hinged upon personal trust and guarantees rather than law, this reliance on a known circle was vital. Operating outside it was risky and difficult. However, the importance of the marketing area stretched far beyond its economic functions. It defined the whole of the peasant's social and cultural life. It was the area to which he looked for entertainment. The theatre, story-telling, restaurants and so forth were all closely associated with the local market. Often this cultural identity was reinforced by variations in the local dialect, or by a special handicraft or folk art only practised within the area. Most marriages took place within its boundaries and this added to its sense of unity. Those peasants that took an interest in social and political affairs talked and thought in terms of the same area. If a person moved to another place to live, he invariably joined an association of people from his home locality and insisted that after death his body should be returned for burial. This sense of attachment is still very strong and it may have been reinforced by the fact that the modern communes in many cases correspond to the area of these old marketing localities. Nevertheless, this has not prevented the growth of more impersonal national loyalties.

In its drive to transform this society after 1949, the Communist Party had two great advantages. First, it had come to power on the basis of mass peasant support. Its membership and army consisted chiefly of peasants who had joined and fought because they believed that the Party would find an answer to their growing economic and social problems. Secondly, it was able to draw upon its long years of experience in rural base areas. Since the early 1930s the Communist Party had survived because it had learnt to operate successfully in the countryside. It had experimented with different types of land reform and rural organization, keeping in close touch with peasant life. Many valuable lessons had been learnt and by 1949 large areas in north China had already begun to change. The Party thus had a good idea of the policies it wanted to adopt and of some of the ways of achieving them.

Reform and Revolution

The first objective after 1949 was to carry out the long promised land reform and transfer ownership of land from the landlords to their tenants. Throughout this process, the Party put great stress on the active participation of the peasants. Party workers encouraged the poorest peasants of a village to discuss amongst themselves their sufferings under the landlords. Their feelings aroused, these activists then formed the nucleus of a peasant association which held large public meetings so that everyone could 'speak out his bitterness'. Next the association tried to determine the class status of the villagers according to the Party's definitions. This was done by public discussion, and took a long time since it had great implications both for the amount of land a family would get and for a family's future political status. Even today families are still referred to by the social classification they were given at that time. The absentee landlords were easily dealt with but the small differences between the remaining families often complicated the issue. Many villages revised their list several times before reaching a satisfactory classification. The peasants then subjected the landlords to a final public denunciation and their lands and property were divided according to an agreed system of allocation based on the average landholding of the area. Some landlords also received a share, though the treatment of them was often rough, particularly in areas where they had collaborated with the Japanese. In many cases the peasants avenged their former suffering by sentencing the landlord to death.

While the economic impact of the reform was important for individual families, in national terms it meant far less. Its main achievement was to redistribute wealth from the rich to the poor. It did not lead to any improvement in agricultural methods and thus provide a long-term means of raising total output. There was still a general shortage of tools, farm animals and credit. The economy functioned more or less as it always had. However, the political impact of the reform was much more important. For the first time in their lives the ordinary peasants had played an active and united role in smashing the landlord class. In doing so the focus of power shifted from the rich to the poor. The reform also began to undermine the traditional order by cutting across the ties of lineage and friendship. As a result, large numbers of peasants came to identify their interests with the power of the Communist Party.

Immediately after land reform, the Party began to develop systems of ownership and management more socialist in character. It warned that if no changes were made the old system of debt and tenancy could easily return. Plans to increase production depended on the greater efficiency of collective organisation and on the improved use of traditional techniques combined with large amounts of intensive manual labour. The first stage was directly copied from wartime experience. Groups of 6 to 10 families joined together as mutual aid teams. They kept private ownership of land but pooled their tools and labour. Each plot was worked in turn and records were kept so that each family benefitted equally. In some cases the peasants bought new animals and tools collectively. In theory membership was voluntary and the more well-off tended not to join, being unwilling to share their advantages with the less fortunate. But official pressure resulted in 60 per cent of all peasant households becoming members of mutual aid teams by 1955. A peasant from Liu Ling village in Shensi Province described what happened to Jan Myrdal in *Report from a Chinese Village*:

> In 1949 a labour exchange group was formed. . . . People thought it better to work together, that that made the work easier and that evening came quicker, if several of you were working together, than if you were working quite alone. To begin with the group was not organised on a permanent basis, but there was a direct agreement between the members to exchange their labour. In 1951 we decided to reorganize the group and put it on a permanent basis as a labour group for mutual help (mutual aid team). . . . The work went well, but there were lots of quarrels about whose land should be taken first. It was difficult to solve all these problems. Some said: 'Why should his field be taken first? I've got a heavier crop. It ought to be my turn now.' Whatever we did, this went on; so then we began talking about forming a farmers' cooperative.

In fact many of the pressures to form elementary agricultural producers' cooperatives came from above. Party members promoted the idea in all parts of the country. At the same time the government saw that the existence of cooperatives would greatly simplify the administration of land tax and the compulsory purchase of grain. Model units were widely publicised for others to copy.

Most elementary cooperatives consisted of 30–40 families, who set up a management committee to control all land and resources. The work was divided among production teams which were roughly equivalent to the former mutual aid teams. Members still owned their land, animals and implements, for which they received rent or hire payments. In addition, they retained small plots to work privately, and also got a share of the total harvest in proportion to the amount of work they did. A percentage of the cooperatives' income was not distributed but accumulated for

22 *The 'Iron Girl's Brigade'—a famous team of workers at Dazhai Commune*

investment.

During 1954 and 1955, the number of cooperatives grew slowly. Membership was voluntary and once again the richer peasants resisted joining. However, social pressure, progressive taxation and discrimination in the supply of government services, fertilizer and credit were used to make them change their minds. By the end of 1956, nearly all peasant households had joined. At the same time the cooperatives were reorganised as advanced types consisting of 100–300 families. The elementary cooperatives were absorbed to become production brigades and the production teams remained as before. From the peasants' point of view there was thus an element of continuity since they still worked together in groups that were more or less the same as the original mutual aid teams. But the economic changes were substantial. Ownership of land was transferred to the cooperative without compensation. Draught animals and large implements were purchased at an agreed price and became collective property. The peasants were entirely dependent on the share of the collective harvest they earned through their labour and what they could grow on their private plots.

This transformation required considerable adjustment. Accumulation, investment and management ceased to be a personal concern, with the result that many peasants lost interest in maintaining collective property. Management committees lacked the skills and experience to run large organisations. They also tended to discourage sideline production such as pig rearing, fruit growing, silk production and so forth. Thus, although the peasants had the right to private subsidiary work, they were not able to do as they pleased. While the output of grain increased, there was a decline in other important commercial and industrial crops. Eventually during 1957 the balance between collective and private had to be revised. Management committees returned many animals, trees and implements to private ownership, enlarged private plots, and reintroduced rural free markets. Collectivisation remained the ultimate goal but, for the moment, a more gradual approach was adopted.

These setbacks came at a time of growing conflict within the Communist Party between those who favoured planned development along Soviet lines and those who looked back to the experience gained in Yenan before 1949. Furthermore, the rapid pace of industrial growth had left agriculture far behind and there were increasing strains between the two sectors. Yet employment opportunities in the towns were not growing fast enough to match the increase in population. More jobs and more production had to be created in the countryside. The result was the introduction of people's communes in 1958. These combined further organisational reform with a drive to develop rural industry as a source of wealth for agricultural growth. The keynote was self-reliance on the peasants' own resources. Between August and September 1958, under pressure from the Party, virtually all of China's peasants became commune members.

The new communes were extremely large, incorporating an average of around 4,600 households and in some cases as many as 10–11,000. They combined local government and economic organisation so that both the farming and non-farming population came under their control. They managed all rural economic activity and not just agriculture. Marketing, transport and public services such as communal mess halls, laundries and schools all became commune enterprises. In addition the commune leadership encouraged the peasants to set up small-scale industries such as the famous 'backyard furnaces', which as their name implies attempted for a brief period in 1958 to produce iron and steel from local ores and coal by makeshift methods. Inevitably, the quality of these efforts was often poor. During the first few months, commune organisation was also highly collectivised. All land and implements became public property. In some places even farm houses and household utensils were taken over. The commune management committee controlled and owned everything. The production brigades, equivalent to the former advanced cooperatives, acted as accounting units, and the production teams carried out the actual work. Peasant income was paid in part as free distribution of commune production according to need, and in part as distribution according to the amount of work performed. Initially private plots and subsidiary work were again curtailed. In practice there was a great deal of variation in the details of organization in different communes. Jan Myrdal recorded the comments of one local Party member.

The discussion about forming a people's commune was short. Some people thought it was an unnecessary measure . . . (they) said: 'Why should we change everything again now? Things are going well as they are. It's just unnecessary trouble and complication and doesn't serve any purpose.' But we discussed and made propaganda. The central committee of the Party, of course, had said that we ought to form people's communes. People's communes were supposed to be a more effective employment of manpower, to give greater possibilities for capital investment; with one we should be maintaining the principle of everyone being paid according to the work he did and be able to give more help to those who got into difficulties. We said other things too. After this propaganda work we joined Liu Ling People's Commune. . . .

We had heard about the business of free food. But we didn't think it would be suitable here with us. We simply did not believe in it. We were afraid it would undermine our members' trust in the principle of a day's work as the unit. It would make consumption independent of the work contributed, and we did not think this would work well. . . . with the introduction of the people's commune and the big propaganda campaigns we had during that time, the members' consciousness increased and their sense of responsibility was strengthened so greatly that it became possible to introduce rational social care. . . . Between September 1958 and February 1959, we experimented producing iron by our local method. We have, of course, both coal and iron-ore up in the hills. We built a blast furnace and I was responsible for organizing the work. There were seventy of us working on this. We were given work points as for all other work. But this didn't happen again. I can't remember the exact figure now, but, as far as I can remember, it didn't pay.

The formation of the communes was accompanied by great optimism that the pace of agricultural development would rapidly accelerate. However, within a year many difficulties had emerged. The initial emphasis on large size resulted in unwieldy units with little economic rationale. Inexperienced management and the diversion of labour to uneconomic projects severely affected agricultural output. This was worsened by three years of exceptionally poor harvests. Many peasants resented the extent of collectivisation and the loss of private undertakings. They accused the cadres of 'blowing the communist wind' by attempting a faster transition to communist society than was possible. In addition, hasty local development upset centralised plans.

Between 1959 and 1962, there was considerable reorganisation. The size of the communes was reduced and their number increased from roughly 26,000 to nearly 76,000. This brought many of them back into line with the traditional marketing areas that had existed before 1949. The size of production brigades and production teams also shrank, and ownership of land and economic accounting were transferred to the production teams thus reducing the importance of the commune leadership. Uneconomic projects were abandoned and free distribution stopped. Private plots and subsidiary undertakings were once again reintroduced. The communes were not destroyed but they lost a great deal of their original character.

This failure sharpened debate within the Party. Peng De-huai, then head of the army, openly criticized Mao and was forced to resign in 1959. Nevertheless, Mao also had to give way. In many communes peasants were allowed more scope to farm privately and material incentives were used as a means of increasing production. Mechanisation was given greater emphasis than collectivisation. Despite the success of these policies during the economic recovery after 1962, the dispute was not settled. Mao went on the offensive, arguing that too much individual farming was undermining the socialist economy. He also believed that collectivisation should precede not follow mechanisation. These arguments came to a head in the Cultural Revolution. Mao's victory put a stop to the trend towards more individual farming but there have not been any attempts to revise the commune structure yet again. Agricultural policy still centres on large-scale industrial support, the gradual extension of small-scale industry in the countryside, and the cautious development of collective undertakings by the peasants.

The Commune Today

The commune is now firmly established as the standard unit of China's agriculture. A typical example is Shuang-wang People's Commune which I visited in 1971. Shuang-wang is situated on the rich loess of the Wei River valley near the city of Weinan in Shensi Province. It has a population of more than 16,000 peasants living in 33 villages. The total area is 26,000 mu (about 4,300 acres, 1 mu equals $\frac{1}{6}$ of an acre) and the chief crops are wheat, cotton, corn, sweet potatoes, and vegetables. Most of the land is flat and stretches along the south bank of the river, reaching up to the suburbs of the city. The village houses are built of the same yellowish-brown earth as forms the roads and fields around them. Their rectangular shape and high courtyard walls make them a distinctive feature of the landscape. Sun Guang-xue, the director of the commune revolutionary committee, told me about Shuang-wang and the way it operates. His description, filled out with information from other communes, illustrates the general features of rural life in China.

Like all communes, Shuang-wang has three levels of management; a revolutionary committee, production brigades, and production teams. The revolutionary committee is the official leading body and its chief tasks are administrative and supervisory. The 11 production brigades help the committee to implement its policies. They do much of the production planning for the production teams under their control, and they each own a number of collective enterprises. The 63 production teams are subdivisions of the brigades. They own the land, do the farming, and are the basic accounting units. Although the production brigades often cooperate on large projects, they are administratively independent of each other. There are many differences between them due to the variety of their natural endowments and to the different collective enterprises they have developed. Those farming hilly land, for example, are poorer than those farming richer land closer to the river. Attempts to equalize income between brigades by getting the richer ones to subsidize the poorer ones

23 *Liu Shu-xian's brigade leadership from Shuangwang Commune. Liu is fourth from left. Sun Guang-xue is second from right*

have so far been resisted by the peasants and are officially regarded as premature. The same differences can be found between
the production teams within a production brigade, though they
are less marked. It is often possible for peasants in one team to have
slightly higher incomes than those in the neighbouring team.

Sun Guang-xue's revolutionary committee has 25 members
who are nominally elected by a congress of peasant representatives
from the brigades. However, most of them are proposed and
approved by the authorities at county level. They include cadres
and peasant representatives. They are paid a salary by the
government and, unlike the ordinary peasant commune members
do not receive a share in the distribution of the commune's
production. Sun explained that he had been transferred to
Shuang-wang in 1970. Previously he had been the director of a
commune to the north.

The close contact between the revolutionary committee and the
local government enables it to act as the link between the county
authorities and the production brigades. The commune leaders
receive instructions from above and report back on developments
in the commune. In addition, the county government regularly

sends down cadres to inspect the work of the revolutionary committee and to explain new policies. The committee also carries out a number of governmental activities within the commune. On behalf of the authorities, it assists in the local management of such things as the tax office, the branch of the People's Bank, and the public granaries. One of its cadres oversees the small free markets where peasants can trade in their private produce. He ensures that official price limits are maintained and issues licences to regular pedlars. Law and order on the commune is looked after by the committee's public security cadre, who as part of his work is closely associated with the county public security hierarchy. The same man runs the commune militia. The revolutionary committee also collects population records, controls the movement of people by issuing travel permits, and keeps a register of births, deaths, and marriages. It takes a small fee from the peasants for doing some of these things.

In contrast to its governmental role, the economic power of the commune leadership is now considerably reduced compared to the early days in 1958. Its chief remaining duty is to ensure that the production plans of the brigades match the demands made on the commune by the state. The commune has to pay a fixed amount of agricultural tax, usually around 5 to 10 per cent of production. It has to supply an annual quota of grain and other crops for compulsory purchase by the state. This varies from 10 to 30 per cent of the crop depending on what is grown and the productivity of the land. It also has to cooperate with the general agricultural plans of the county such as large-scale irrigation projects or road-building. The revolutionary committee complies with these demands by suggesting production targets for the various crops to each brigade. The brigade leaders then discuss these figures with the team leaders and at public meetings before negotiating any amendments and reaching a final agreement. After these arrangements have been made, the brigade and team leaders are free to decide between themselves the best ways to meet their targets. They can decide what additional crops they will grow, how they will dispose of them, how much they will accumulate and how much they will consume. Many of the final decisions are, in fact, made by the team leaders, particularly those on accumulation and consumption. In the process, the Party and commune leaders exert great pressure to make them abide by overall economic and political aims. Propaganda in the media explains official policy, and this is backed up by adjustments in price levels to encourage the planting of particular crops.

The commune revolutionary committee runs a number of offices to give advice and help. These are devoted to such things as production, finance, commerce, grain management, welfare, political work and public security. The cadres in charge of these offices check up on the relevant aspects of the work of the brigades. They make sure mistakes aren't made and they help improve the quality of the management. They also coordinate projects that required cooperation between a number of brigades, such as road maintenance, transport and irrigation works. The communes commercial services are a good example. Each brigade has a supply and marketing cooperative which runs a small shop selling daily necessities and farm supplies. It also buys part of the output of the peasants' private plots and sideline activities and some of the surplus production of the brigade. The work is supervised by one of the brigade leaders. However, the shop gets its supplies from the commune's central supply and marketing cooperative. This makes the general buying and selling policies in accordance with the state plans, and it runs a bigger shop which carries a larger stock of goods.

The only economic enterprises owned collectively by the whole commune are those too large or expensive for individual brigades to undertake. Shuang-wang does not have any of these but examples on other communes include such things as lorry and tractor stations, relatively well-equipped machine workshops, small mines, large-scale handicraft workshops and small local hospitals. The commune revolutionary committee's finances depend on its income from these enterprises and the miscellaneous administrative charges levied on the brigades. For major new projects, it needs extra support from the brigades, or it obtains a bank loan or county subsidy.

Finally, Sun Guang-xue stressed the political work of the commune leadership. In accordance with the principle of 'unified leadership', he is both director of the revolutionary committee and secretary of the Commune Party Committee. In addition, 13 of his 25 colleagues on the revolutionary committee are also Party members. This ensures that commune decision-making is subordinate to Party control. The Party branch

organisations at brigade level are similarly related to the brigade leadership. The commune also has the usual mass organisations open to non-Party members which turn to the Party for guidance. These include the Communist Youth League for the young, the Poor and Lower-middle Peasants' Association which meets regularly to discuss all aspects of commune work, and the Women's Association which deals specifically with the position of women and policies towards them, such as equal rights, adherence to the new Marriage Law, and advice on birth control. The Commune Party Committee relies on the public discussions and propaganda work of these bodies to publicise its aims and to gather the ideas and criticisms of the commune members. While the final decisions are taken within the power structure, this feedback mechanism can be an important way in which the peasants are able to voice their opinions and influence events.

A Brigade at Work

The brigade leaders of Shuang-wang Commune are mainly local peasants elected by representatives from the teams and approved in their posts by the commune revolutionary committee. Liu Shu-xian is one of Shuang-wang's most successful brigade leaders and, as the story in Chapter 1 shows, he has achieved national fame as a model. However, his personal history is typical of many of China's peasant cadres. Liu's family were originally poor peasants and they lost their land before 1949. They had to work as labourers and supplemented their income by begging. Eventually his father died and his mother was forced to sell his two sisters and younger brother. During land reform, Liu received a share of land and became leader of a mutual aid team. In 1952 he joined the Communist Party and was subsequently made director of the local elementary cooperative. He continued in this position as the cooperative expanded and was eventually appointed brigade leader and Party branch secretary when the commune was set up in 1958. As well as doing administrative work for the brigade, he spends much of his time labouring in the fields. For his constant support for collective agriculture he has been given the title 'national advanced worker in agriculture' and he has many commendations on his office wall, including one signed by Zhou En-lai. As well as himself, there are 10 others on the brigade revolutionary committee, each one specializing in certain aspects of the brigade work.

When the commune was first set up, Liu's brigade had 120 households. There are now 347, thanks partly to the inclusion of some suburban areas of the nearby city and partly to the influx of people sent down from the towns to work in the countryside. The total population has therefore risen from 600 to 1,800 and the number of production teams from 2 to 7. The area farmed by the brigade is 2574 *mu* (429 acres), of which in 1971, 1480 *mu* were devoted to wheat, 695 to cotton, and the rest to corn, sweet potatoes, fruit and vegetables. Liu said that before collectivisation, the grain yield per *mu* had been around 200 *jin* (100 kilos, 1 *jin* equals $\frac{1}{2}$ kilo). Since 1965 it had averaged 1,100 *jin*. Part of the reason for this increase is due to the work of the brigade's agricultural science research station. This has experimented with and introduced various forms of crop rotation, interplanting and seed selection. It is run by trained technicians and experienced old peasants. As a result of this increased productivity, the teams are now able to keep large reserves and to sell more grain and cotton to the state.

The work of the brigade leaders is important to the teams since they control the collective services and enterprises. Through shrewd investment and good advice, they can directly affect the livelihood of the ordinary peasants. The teams turn to their brigade for such things as the use of tractors, the supply of chemical fertilizer, machine maintenance, and veterinary services. These undertakings are managed and owned by the brigade and built up with funds from the teams, whose needs they are meant to serve. Liu's brigade has a number of them. There is a veterinary clinic which cares for the teams' pigs, chickens, and 140 draught animals, as well as the brigade's 20 dairy cows. The latters' milk is sold through commercial channels in Weinan city since most peasants don't drink it. The brigade's mechanised ploughing team has two tractors and equipment for processing cotton. When not ploughing the tractors are used for heavy transport. Maintenance of this equipment and of that of the teams is carried out in the brigade machine repair shop which has a couple of simple lathes and employs 4 blacksmiths and 4 carpenters. There is also a clothing workshop which employs 4 tailors, a small brick and tile factory, and an afforestation unit which looks after its 40–50,000 trees.

Brigade income is made up of the earnings from these enterprises, the charges made to teams for administrative work, and the funds contributed by the teams for welfare and investment. The money collected in these ways has to pay the wages of the people employed by the brigade and all its running costs. Any excess is partly invested in further collective enterprises and partly distributed to the teams for their own use. It also pays for the welfare services. Liu's brigade runs a primary school for children and literacy classes for adults. It has special funds to help out the old and infirm and to assist families in an emergency. Widows, for example, are guaranteed a home, food and clothing. In addition, there is a credit cooperative which can make loans to teams and to individuals. A cultural centre with a reading room and a team of amateur singers and dancers provides entertainment. These preserve the local styles of folk singing. Occasionally the brigade also arranges a visit by a touring film unit. Health is looked after by brigade medical orderlies called 'barefoot doctors' who use both Chinese and western medicine. Difficult cases go to the commune clinic and can be referred to the hospital in Weinan. Liu's brigade pays all the medical fees of its peasants. In other brigades, the costs are either shared between the brigade and the peasant, or else a form of medical insurance is used.

The brigade is an important body in the eyes of most peasants. However, Liu Shu-xian made it clear that the production team is the basic collective unit. The ordinary commune members have more to do with their team leaders than with any other of the commune cadres.

The Teams that do the Work

The production teams own the land, water resources and other means of production including small machines, farm animals and large farm implements. They are also independent accounting units, each one being responsible for its own profit and loss. Each team is led by a group of 5 people, once again elected by the commune members but subject to higher approval. One of them represents the Party and is in charge of political work. The others look after production, accounting, militia work, and women's affairs. This group liaises with the brigade leaders, organises the farming work, and presides over the distribution of income.

On average each of the teams in Liu's brigade has 50 households with a total of 250 people, figures much the same as those for teams throughout China. There are slightly more men than women, and about one-third are under 16. The labour force of each team is roughly 100 men and women, but almost everyone is able to do some paid work during the year. The average able-bodied man spends 300 days per year working on the team lands. He gets 4 days off a month, and a week or two during the New Year Festival, which is celebrated according to the lunar calendar. The slack agricultural months are November and December, and most of the capital construction—things like well-digging and land levelling—is done during this period. When the weather is very bad, it is impossible to work in the fields and the peasants stay at home, resting or doing private work. The collective working day lasts about 8 hours divided into three sessions. The peasants work on their private plots before and after this and on their days off. Different teams organize their workforce in different ways. Some allocate certain areas of land to certain groups of peasants who do all the work on it. Others set up specialist groups such as ploughers, hoers, weeders, and so forth which move about the team land doing their work.

Team management is conducted in a very open way. There are many public discussions, and the peasants have the chance to put

25 *The dragon-spine water wheel. Traditional methods still play an important role in rural development*

forward their own ideas and to criticise the proposals of the team leaders. The questions that generate the most debate are those of production and of the distribution of income. Production problems centre on the proportion of land to be devoted to each crop. While the national priority is to see sufficient grain and cotton grown, many peasants want to see more land devoted to crops that have a higher market value. The team leaders have to balance these pressures and ensure that self-interest by team members does not clash with collective plans.

The debate over the distribution of team income is once again the result of the need to balance the interests of the state, the collective and the individual. The total income of the team comes from two main sources—its own production, and its share of any dividends from the brigade. Before this can be divided among the peasants, a number of deductions have to be made. First the agricultural tax has to be deducted. Secondly, a part of the crop has to be sold to the state under the compulsory purchase system. The amount varies according to the crop and the productivity of the land, and it can be changed to match harvest conditions. In bad years it can be waived altogether. However, the compulsory purchase quota does not represent a total loss to team income since the state pays for the goods it buys, albeit at a price below that allowed on the free market. Finally, the team has to pay for all the costs of production, including such things as seed, new equipment, repairs, administration expenses, and payments to the brigades for services rendered. After all these deductions, the team is left with about 60 per cent of its original income. It then has to decide how much it will accumulate and how much it will consume. During the public discussion of this question, the cadres generally argue for greater accumulation while the ordinary peasants often prefer greater consumption. The money that is accumulated is put into two funds, one for capital construction and one for welfare. A part of each is controlled by the brigade for the use of all the teams collectively. In most years, these funds account for 15 to 20 per cent of team income. The remainder is then distributed among the peasants in accordance with the work they have done over the year.

Methods of distributing income vary a good deal in detail from one part of China to another. The two standard features found on all communes are the work-point and the labour day. At Shuang-wang, each peasant is awarded work-points on the basis of the type of work he does and the length of time spent doing it. Thus, as a general rule, a man doing a heavy day's work manuring the fields will get more points than one doing light weeding in an afternoon. However, there are often difficulties in determining the work-point value of different types of work and in setting the standards against which to measure performance. For example, should the points awarded for hoeing be the same as those awarded for threshing? Or should the points given to an older and weaker man for digging be the same as those given to a younger and stronger man? Problems like these are handled in two stages. First the team accountant keeps a record of the actual work done by each peasant. Then at regular intervals open meetings are held to assess the work-points due to each individual for the work he has done. This is decided according to the individual's abilities and according to some generally accepted ideas of what the standard rate for the job should be. Any problems or complaints that arise are settled by public debate. Sometimes the points awarded to an individual might also be adjusted to take account of his attitude towards his work and his level of commitment to the Communist Party—an approach which gives further impetus to spreading the Party's ideas in the countryside. However, moves during the Cultural Revolution to make this a central feature of the work-point system have since been criticised for undermining the principle of 'to each according to his work'. Once a peasant's work-points have been settled, they are added up and converted into labour days at the rate of 10 points per day. At the end of the year, the team accountant takes the total distributable income and divides it by the total number of labour days performed by all the members of the team. In this way, he arrives at a money value for each labour day. The peasants are then paid according to the number of labour days they have worked during the year. The value of a labour day can vary from harvest to harvest and from team to team. In Liu's brigade in 1971 some teams paid 0·80 *yuan* and others paid 1·00 *yuan* or more.

The actual payment to the peasants is made partly in cash and partly in kind. It is issued in two stages, the first in spring and the second in autumn. Advance payments can be drawn if necessary. Part of the distribution in kind is looked upon as a basic subsistence allowance. It is paid to all peasants, even if they have not done all the labour days necessary. The rest all depends on work done. At Shuang-wang in 1971, the average per capita distribution was 450 *jin* of grain, 2 *jin* of raw cotton and 17·5 feet of cotton cloth. Other goods supplied included meat, vegetables, fuel and cooking oil. The cash value of these goods came to around 70 *yuan* per family. Cash income for the average healthy working man was 280 *yuan*. Individuals received more or less, according to their abilities. In terms of the total population of the brigade, the value of all income received from the collective was 120 *yuan* per head. However, this average figure disguises the fact that families with a lot of labour power were able to earn much more than those with very little.

Apart from this income from the collective, the peasants of Shuang-wang can also make money from subsidiary work and by growing things on their private plots. Subsidiary work includes weaving baskets and hats from straw, making clothes, raising pigs, chickens and ducks, gathering medicinal herbs, and so forth. The products of these activities can be sold to the brigade supply and marketing cooperative, or on the free market. The private plots are part of the team's land but are given over to the peasants for their own use. Every commune member is entitled to a plot, no matter what his age, but there is usually a limit on what one family can have. Plot size depends on the type of land and the decisions of the team but, as a general rule, they must not take up more than 5 per cent of the team's total farm land. In Liu Shu-xian's brigade, 3 teams have a standard plot size of 0·1 *mu* and the other four have 0·14 *mu*. The peasants grow vegetables, food for their animals, or crops they can sell in the market. The manure used on the plots comes from the peasants' own lavatories and from their animals. It is the amount left over after the collective has been supplied with the fixed quota per animal which the peasants have to provide, and for which they are paid in work-points. The food value of the private plot is fairly important since it provides peasants with a source of fresh vegetables, but Liu calculates that the per capita money income from it is only about 10 *yuan*, or less than 10 per cent of the income from the collective. In poorer communes where the labour day is worth less, the value of the private plot may be proportionately higher. In the economy as a whole, the peasants' subsidiary work and plots help to supply rural markets with goods, the towns with vegetables and eggs, and industry with some of its raw materials such as tobacco and pig products.

Stresses and Strains in Commune Life

Although the commune structure as it exists at Shuang-wang has gradually achieved a good deal of stability during its 16 years of life, there are still many underlying problems. Most of them centre either on maintaining an acceptable balance between the collective economy and permissible private undertakings, or on correctly defining the relationship between different levels of management. Since the Party always emphasises the collective, cadres are wary of making decisions which might render them liable for criticism for encouraging capitalist tendencies or for being solely interested in profits. At the same time, experience has shown that if the peasants are not allowed to do some private work, their enthusiasm is dampened and there is a decline in rural markets and peasant income. The following examples from the Chinese media show how such problems arise and how they are ideally dealt with.

In October 1972, a commune in Fukien Province reported that it had just resolved a long debate over the way to meet the demands of both the collective and the individual. It appears that during the latter stages of the Cultural Revolution, a number of cadres had attempted to raise the level of ownership from the team to the brigade. They had also taken into collective ownership all the fruit trees privately cultivated by the peasants. The result was a loss of peasant confidence and a drop in fruit production. Eventually the County Party Committee advised the commune cadres that they should observe the national policy on commune structure and at the same time encourage the peasants to undertake legitimate domestic sidelines. Some of the cadres felt that the county authorities were being conservative rather than progressive, but the latter countered by saying that it was following the Party's policies, which were the correct way to build socialism. Regarding the peasants' fruit trees, the County Party Committee argued: 'It is proper and permissible. It can increase social wealth, and increase the commune members' income at the same time. It can enhance the socialist education of the commune members, increase their initiative to farm for the revolution, and will not affect the collective production.' Thus, despite the theoretical stress on socialism, the committee in practise allowed the peasants some scope for private enterprise.

A similar problem arose around the same time at a commune in Kirin Province. This concerned the right of craftsmen such as blacksmiths, carpenters and masons to do work outside their own production brigades. A commune regulation had been drawn up during the Cultural Revolution forbidding them to do outside jobs since this might lead them to 'take the capitalist road'. Apparently, before the Cultural Revolution these craftsmen had been free to go and work where they wanted to, and they had neglected the collective, only caring about their own income. In the spring of 1972, the brigade leaders began allowing them to do outside jobs again. After some debate, the Commune Party Committee decided that this cancellation of the regulation should be allowed to stand, and the relationship between the collective and the individual should be defined afresh. 'For the jobs they perform outside, their work-points will be calculated by their own production teams according to their respective kinds of crafts and their skills, and according to criteria somewhat higher than those for the average commune members. As for the income they get for the jobs they perform outside, the larger part of it should be turned over to the production team with the smaller portion going to themselves as compensation for wear and tear on their equipment and so on.'

A final example from Liaoning Province in January 1973 illustrates a different kind of problem. During the previous three winters, the communes in a county had been carrying out extensive capital construction, digging wells and irrigation channels and building dams. However, the commune cadres had at first allocated work tasks and investment demands to the brigades in a very arbitrary manner. As a result, brigades which did not benefit greatly from the schemes found themselves contributing the same or even more effort than those that received a large return. Enthusiasm for the project declined and the work moved ahead very slowly. Finally the County Party Committee called a meeting of commune cadres and insisted that the principles of voluntary participation and equal benefit should be adhered to. Thereafter, they 'allocated (demands for) manpower and funds among the brigades according to the benefits they respectively received, and gave reasonable rewards to those brigades which took part in the project but did not receive any benefit from it.' In this way the relationship between the different collective units was harmonised.

While most of the reports in the Chinese media reflect problems like the above and show how they were solved, occasionally examples are found of corrupt cadres who embezzle funds or use the collective organization for their own profit. Cases like these are not publicised, but secret documents stolen by Nationalist troops in 1963 showed that they are dealt with by official enquiry and punishment.

The Peasant at Home

The transformation of rural institutions since 1949 has considerably changed the way of life of the peasant family. Whatever misgivings there might remain about the disappearance of private ownership, the past 25 years have undoubtedly seen a more equal sharing of wealth in the Chinese countryside. The standard of living has risen and the commune organisation has channelled growing social benefits to the peasants. There is now much greater dependence on the collective in many areas of daily life.

Family income comes from collective work and from small private undertakings. Social pressure and commune regulations ensure that the collective comes first. Peasants who try to concentrate exclusively on their own sidelines face legal restrictions

26 *Meals are often eaten outdoors. In Dazhai the peasants work early and late but take a long lunch break*

and may be subjected to political criticism. Large families with many able workers can exploit both sources of income more effectively than smaller families. However, in all families the old, the young and even the infirm try to do some work for the collective in order to raise family income, or do the household chores so that the better workers can get out to work. Many families also have members working in commune and brigade enterprises, or in city factories. The wages earned in this way are higher than the return from working in agriculture and such jobs are eagerly sought after.

The largest single family expense is the house. This is owned by the family and paid for out of savings or by a loan from the brigade. The cost can be around two or three years' wages for the average healthy man. There has been a great deal of building and re-building of rural housing since 1949 but the styles are still very traditional. Once the house is built, the cost of upkeep is very low. Apart from electricity, if supplied, there are no standing charges. Clothing is in part provided for by the cotton distributed by the teams. Any other needs have to be bought from the commune shop. While machine-made cloth is replacing homespun, it is rare for the peasants to spend their money on ready-made clothes. Usually the women do the tailoring and they also make shoes from cotton or hemp and weave straw or bamboo-hats and raincoats. However, rubber shoes and plastic coats are becoming very popular and most families now spend some money on them.

Fuel for heating and cooking is obtained from leftovers such as rice stalks or corn cobs after the grain has been removed. Sometimes communes have small coalmines and distribute coal, or exploit trees for wood. Fuel the family gets in this way forms part of earned income. Food comes almost entirely from the collective or private plot. Very little is bought in the market apart from salt, vinegar, spices, and luxuries such as sugar and sweets. Since there are no laws about making wines and spirits, it is easy for the peasants to make their own. However, drinking alcohol is generally frowned upon except on special occasions or among older men. Top favourites are strong white spirits made from grain.

Although the traditional attachment to the family and locality lingers on, the commune structure has made it difficult to fulfil old obligations. Relatives can no longer be easily granted favours or given jobs. Market operations do not depend so much on personal contacts and they are carried out through new administrative bodies. For such things as medical services, welfare, entertainment, and education, the peasants now rely on the commune and not the lineage. But within families some traditions remain strong. While youthful rebellion and technical expertise have both challenged the traditional social status enjoyed by old age, the family elders still claim respect and honour, and make many of the important decisions. Although women have made great

27 *A peasant housewife's kitchen*

progress in their fight for social equality, men have not lost all their advantages and boys are still preferred to girls. Despite the Marriage Law, arranged marriages are not unknown. Methods of bringing children up follow old customs and many of the babies seen on communes are dressed and groomed in the way that old superstitions demand. It will take time for many of these things to die out and be replaced by new traditions. Despite the great changes that have come about, old cultural patterns persist and influence the new.

4
City Life

China has one of the largest urban populations in the world. Around 130 million people live in its cities and towns, working in industry, commerce, administration, education and culture. Since 1949, China's leaders have devoted considerable resources to building up new industrial centres, expanding old, and improving the quality of urban life. Through their industries and services, the cities have come to play a key role in the struggle for economic development. However, the Chinese insist that the cities should not monopolise the wealth and social services of the country. Industry should serve agriculture, and every effort should be made to prevent urban living standards rising too far above the general level of the countryside. At various times, the Communist Party has mounted campaigns to send doctors, teachers, administrators and other specialists out of the cities to spread their talents among rural society. It has also tried to stop the movement of people from the countryside to the towns, and to slow down the rate of urban population growth. The declared aim of these drives is to destroy the 'three major differences', those between town and country, between worker and peasant, and between mental and manual labour. Thus, despite the many advantages of city life, the Chinese are concerned to maintain a balance between urban and rural society. The cities must provide leadership and the means of modernisation but they should not reap all the rewards.

Revolution comes to Town

Revolutionary ideas and modern technology first came to China through cities along its coast, opened for foreign settlement and trade by force of arms during the nineteenth century. At first the new society that began to grow in the 'treaty ports' was dominated by foreign powers and it failed to mature in its urban setting. It was not until the 1930's when the Communist Party retreated to its rural bases that the revolutionary forces born in the city were effectively adapted to the Chinese reality. The Communists did not return to the cities until the moment of victory in 1949. In their eyes, the cities were corrupt centres of imperialist control and capitalist ideology. They were determined to carry out a thorough transformation.

On coming to power, the Communists inherited two very different kinds of city. Most of those in the interior had remained relatively untouched by foreign influence. Their physical appearance underlined their traditional origins. High city walls towered over low houses. All the streets ran north to south and east to west, dominated by the prominent buildings of the past such as the offices of the Imperial bureaucracy, the Confucian temples and the old markets. Although many of these cities had once been great commercial centres with rich merchant families and large artisan classes, they had not achieved the political and economic independence that characterised the 'treaty ports' along the coast. By 1949, the long years of war had led to decline and had cut many of them off from the rural society they had once served. Instead they had become centres of refuge for absentee landlords and merchants, consuming the products of the countryside but giving very little in return. The Communists had to start from scratch to build up new industries and urban services.

By contrast, the largest and most modern cities were those that had been centres of foreign power. They had much in common with other large cities throughout the world. In Shanghai, tall, western-style buildings dominated the skyline, lorries, trams and cars filled the streets, extensive industrial areas created their own strange landscape, and the suburban districts had neat rows of houses standing in tidy gardens. Many of these things remain today and vividly recall the imperialist impact on China before 1949. The centre of gravity in these cities had moved to new commercial districts which housed the head offices of large banks, trading companies and industrial manufacturers. Urban services such as schools, hospitals, telephones, sewers, running water and

public services had been introduced with varying degrees of success. But the best of city life was under foreign control and only foreigners and rich Chinese could enjoy it. Huge numbers of people had little opportunity for employment and lived in slums or were homeless. Shanghai provided the most extreme example. In 1935, 5,590 corpses were removed from the streets of the foreign-policed areas alone. Two years later this figure rose to 20,746. Crime and corruption were so rife that brothel-keeping and kidnapping were major commercial undertakings. The contrast between wealth and poverty was immense and the over-whelming drive to obtain a quick profit created little sense of social responsibility. Cities like these presented the Communists with many tough social problems for urgent solution.

Urban industry also needed careful handling. Before 1949, its total annual output never rose above 10·5 per cent of the net domestic product. When the Communists took over, even this low proportion had declined thanks to the war and a staggering rate of inflation. Foreign competition, investment and control had not worked in China's best interests. Most of the factories produced consumer goods such as cotton textiles, cigarettes, matches and processed foodstuffs. There was little investment in heavy industry. Nearly all machinery and vital raw materials like steel had to be imported. Foreign control had also distorted the pattern of industrial growth. Most modern industry was concentrated along the east coast and in the northeast. Shanghai had half of all China's mechanised factories. The transport networks did not serve the nation as a whole but mainly these coastal centres. Furthermore, most of the goods produced by industry were sold in urban markets. Although agricultural products were important to the cities, the rural economy absorbed little of the industrial output in return. There was no rural market capable of stimulating greater industrial growth.

This general situation was compounded by the poor quality of management, particularly in Chinese-owned factories. Short-term profit seeking and speculative investment in commodities had diverted funds from badly needed modernisation and expansion. Relations between managers and shareholders, foremen and workmen tended to be based on traditional ideas of loyalty and obligation rather than on impersonal standards of efficiency, expertise, wages and costs. Inevitably there was much exploitation, with women and children being forced to work long hours in poor conditions for low pay. This created a great deal of social misery. It also prevented the growth of a skilled, stable labour force since workers could get little return from their employment. Thus, the Communists not only had to restore the economy and stop inflation, but they also had to carry out important industrial reforms. The cities gave them immense economic and political advantages but they first had to learn how to use them and how to overcome the many immediate problems.

The Socialist Transformation

The first priority in 1949 was to consolidate the control of the cities gained by military occupation and to get everything working again. In most places, Military Affairs Control Commissions took over, combining Army and Party leadership. These commissions dealt firmly with political and economic resistance to the new regime and clamped down severely on all crime. In other matters they were more flexible and pragmatic. Task forces were set up to handle special problems. Ordinary officials, businessmen and managers were encouraged to return to their posts to carry on their work more or less as usual, subject to the directives and scrutiny of the new power-holders. The less politically sensitive the work and the greater the need for technical skill, the less the Communists interferred with existing arrangements. However, Party activity and recruitment in the cities gradually expanded, and eventually a more formal Party and government structure was established. Municipal offices with bureaus for such things as public security, commerce, education, industry, and employment replaced the Commissions. By 1952, general economic recovery had largely been achieved and the Party was in a position to begin its drive for 'socialist transformation'. This consisted of the socialisation of the economy by the transfer of industrial and commercial ownership and management to the state, and the reorganisation of social institutions to match the new economic and political structure. The inefficiency and corruption of the preceeding Nationalist government had created a lot of public goodwill towards the Communists, and even capitalists supported many of their reforms. But the Party lacked the experience, personnel and skills to realise its aims. It therefore adopted two central strategies. On the one hand, it envisaged a period of transition during which capitalists would be allowed to go on operating, and on the other, it set out to import ideas, experience and methods from the Soviet Union.

Toleration of some form of capitalism had long been a declared part of the Communists' plans for social development after gaining power. This policy had gained them much support in the fight against the Nationalists. After 1949, Communist propaganda continued to stress the beneficial aspects of some private enterprise. The new government set the limits, but it still left scope for the capitalist to work. However, new laws about working hours and conditions, welfare benefits, trade union rights, wages, interest and profit rates, and foreign trading all changed the environment within which the private capitalist operated. Moreover, many of the major industries, public utilities and transport services were already under state control, influencing the general functioning of the economy. At the same time a programme of worker participation in management and political mobilisation of workers

29 *Women are encouraged to play an important part in factory life*

through the trade unions was begun, which undermined the position of the capitalists. These developments came to a head in two campaigns of late 1951 and early 1952.

The first of these was the 'three anti' campaign which opposed the three evils of corruption, waste and excessive red tape in the Party and government. Some of these failings were the result of the Party's own inexperience. Others were caused by pre-1949 bureaucrats refusing to change their style of working. In Shanghai, for example, over 95 per cent of officials from the Nationalist period had stayed at their posts. The second campaign was the 'five anti' which attacked capitalists for the five crimes of bribery, tax evasion, theft of state property, cheating on government contracts, and stealing state economic secrets. The Party intensified propaganda work and political organisation among the workers. The latter then held mass meetings at which they criticised their bosses for their alleged crimes. They also put up posters in the streets and formed investigation teams to examine the evidence. However, very few businessmen were finally imprisoned. The government chiefly imposed financial penalties, either as fines or as demands for the repayment of tax. Since this weakened many firms and forced them to take out government loans, the end result was greater government control. In addition, new policies for allocating contracts, raw materials and markets further limited private enterprise.

Whatever the real extent of the capitalists' guilt, these campaigns foreshadowed the end of the mixed economy. In the years that followed, the expansion of the state-owned industries rapidly eroded the importance of the private sector. Between 1952 and 1955, the output value of private industry fell from 32 per cent to 16 per cent of total industrial output. The capitalists had to defer to the Party organisations and trade unions in their factories and could do little without prior approval. Finally, in 1956, all private businesses that had not already done so were converted into joint state-private concerns. This transferred ownership and management to the state and left the capitalists as state employees with salaries and a right to draw a fixed interest of 5 per cent on the value of their original capital investment. Some of the richer capitalists were able to maintain their position as millionaires right up until 1966, though they had no real economic power and little use for their money beyond consumption. Despite the criticisms of capitalists voiced during the Cultural Revolution, there has been no public announcement that their rights have been officially withdrawn.

The reorganisation of private industry also led to its rationalisation within the state system. Enterprises of the same kind were united into single corporations and many were integrated into existing organisations. The process also affected many small private traders, pedlars and handicraft workers. They were organised into cooperatives. As members of cooperatives, they owned and controlled their new units collectively. Subject to legal and political pressures, they could make most of their own decisions about accumulation and consumption.

While this policy towards private enterprise was gradually evolving, the other strategy of reliance on Soviet methods and Soviet aid was also becoming a major feature of urban and industrial development. In part this alignment with the Soviet Union was caused by the western embargo on trade and diplomatic relations, despite China's willingness to maintain some contacts. However, political affinity between the two countries was very strong. The Chinese borrowed heavily from the Russians in almost every field, ranging from methods of organization such as the structure of government, factory management and school administration to particular techniques such as cost accounting, engineering design and machine construction. During the 1950s, they translated large numbers of books and articles from Russian and sent many thousands of students to Soviet universities. Over the same period, experts went to China from the Soviet Union and other communist countries to work with and train the Chinese. Russian faces and machinery soon became a familiar part of the city scene.

The greatest experiment with Soviet methods was the First Five-Year Plan from 1953 to 1957. At its heart was a drive to double industrial output through the development of 694 key enterprises, of which the most vital 156 were designed, funded and built by the Soviet Union. They included complete iron and steel complexes, metallurgical plants, coal mines, chemical works, power stations and many kinds of machine tool plants. Their completion eventually enabled China to produce motor vehicles, tractors, locomotives, aeroplanes and a wide variety of industrial goods out of domestic resources. Nearly all of this investment was

30 *Slogans call for more worker participation in management at the Shanghai Machine Tool Plant*

directed at inland cities rather than the already industrialised centres along the coast. Places like Wuhan, Paotow, Lanchow, Chengchow and Loyang became major manufacturing centres. The Plan was less comprehensively organised than the Soviet equivalents but it embodied most of the characteristics of the Soviet approach to economic growth. Its major emphasis was on heavy industry, particularly iron and steel, coal, cement and electricity. Light industry and agriculture were neglected by comparison. It had a preference for completely centralised control so that each stage was coordinated through the central ministries and their agencies at provincial level. Little scope was left for innovation and initiative from below. As a whole, it relied on large-scale, capital-intensive investment rather than small-scale, labour-intensive investment. Finally, it had a strong bias towards technical expertise in decision-making. Political values received much less attention.

Despite year to year fluctuations and delayed completion of some of the largest projects, the Plan achieved most of its targets. Heavy industrial output rose rapidly and a large amount of new industrial capacity was created. However, there were also many problems. Lack of coordination between projects led to bottle-necks in the supply of materials and power. Although the concentration on heavy industry created an indispensable base for all economic growth, it did not immediately supply goods that would help increase agricultural output. In addition, the emphasis on industrial growth within cities accentuated urban-rural differences. Wage levels, social services and living standards remained far higher in the cities, and there was a tendency for people to drift in from the countryside. The reliance on technical experts, who were essential to handle the complexities of centralised planning and modern technology, reduced the importance of political values in decision-making and in promotion. The relative neglect of light industry and agriculture depressed the market in consumer goods and caused shortages of industrial crops and of foodstuffs in the cities. Rationing of cotton cloth was introduced in 1954 and of grain in 1955. Although wages were rising, there was little to spend the money on. Furthermore, capital-intensive heavy industry did not provide enough employment to match the rate of population growth. The number of unemployed and underemployed in the cities began to rise. Some of these problems were the inevitable result of economic growth but others were inherent in the approach adopted. The Chinese therefore began to question the applicability of the Soviet model to the Chinese situation—a reappraisal which contributed to the Sino-Soviet split. It also added to the growing political divisions within the Communist Party, divisions that were already causing debate over agricultural policy and a wide range of social issues. Most

31 *Buses, cars and modern buildings still give China's cities advantages over the countryside. A bridge at Shanghai*

leaders agreed that some modification of policy was necessary but Mao Ze-dong and his supporters preferred a complete change.

'The Great Leap Forward' — A Radical Alternative

'The Great Leap Forward' of 1958 was an attempt to tackle the problems left untouched by the Soviet model. It embraced the whole of social and economic policy and was closely integrated with the introduction of people's communes in the countryside. Mao rejected a strategy for development which concentrated on large-scale capital investment and slow but thorough technical modernisation. Since China lacked both funds and skills, such a strategy implied a slow rate of progress and continuous dependence on foreign aid. Instead, he believed that institutional reform and political mobilisation could generate sufficient savings and initiative to speed up the whole process. He called for a greater balance between heavy and light industry, between large and small enterprises, between capital-intensive and labour-intensive investment, and between modern and traditional techniques. His policy was summed up in the slogan 'walking on two legs'. The campaign for rapid economic growth in the countryside was intended to find a way of absorbing the surplus labour of both the cities and the villages. The decentralisation of control from the ministries in Peking to the provincial authorities was aimed at preventing bureaucratic action from stifling local enthusiasm and at reducing the number of non-productive officials.

In practice, 'The Great Leap Forward' abandoned many of the guidelines of the First Five-Year Plan. Technical and managerial staff had to defer to Party authority; administrative and planning procedures were simplified or put to one side. With the exception of key enterprises, the government handed over some 80 per cent of all industry to provincial and municipal authorities, who also gained the right to retain and use many of the taxes previously forwarded to Peking. Managers within enterprises were allowed to keep more of their profits for investment as they saw fit. Planning became a flexible system of target setting and, since targets were revised continuously by enterprises on their own initiative, centralised coordination became impossible. At the same time, grass-roots innovation and experiment were actively encouraged. Small factories with little mechanisation or capital mushroomed everywhere. During the summer of 1958, the formation of rural communes stimulated the introduction of of urban communes which also aimed to integrate all economic and social activity in one unit. In areas dominated by one mine or one large factory, some success was achieved. But in more diverse city districts, things didn't go so well. Eventually the urban communes disappeared.

Although 1958 saw a shift of investment towards light industry and support for agriculture and a great increase in industrial production, there was also much waste and a marked decline in the quality of output. Over-ambitious plans combined with the neglect of technical considerations led to shortages of raw materials and transport bottlenecks. Too many new projects were started without concern for profitability which would finance further growth. The lack of coordination made it difficult for the central government to correct mistakes. The result was a severe industrial crisis compounded by the bad harvests of 1959 to 1961 and by the sudden withdrawal of Soviet aid and technicians in 1960. The problems considerably strengthened the hand of those within the Party who preferred a more cautious technical approach, and Mao had to give way.

During the years of recovery that followed, the government and Party reintroduced greater central control with an emphasis on careful, technical development. Manipulation of prices, profits and incentives again became more important than political mobilisation and the Party cadres therefore had to return some decision-making power to the hands of technical experts. Local initiative in projects of uncertain profitability was actively discouraged. However, the disappearance of Soviet help and the absence of capital funds made a simple reversion to former policies impossible. In addition, most of China's leaders agreed that a better balance between heavy and light industry and between modern and traditional techniques was desirable. They also recognised the need to give priority to producing goods for agriculture like fertilizer and agricultural machinery.

Nevertheless, the underlying dispute remained unsolved. Mao believed that the 'professional' approach was neglecting potentials that could be tapped by political mobilisation, and it was creating social inequality by giving the cities an advantage over the countryside. He feared a loss of revolutionary purpose through the emergence of an urban-based technical and bureaucratic elite.

95

As in other matters, the Cultural Revolution was a turning point in the debate. Mao's victory enabled him to reassert his ideas once again. However, this time the haste and inexperience of 1958 has been replaced by a greater concern for coordination and practical efficiency.

Inside the Factory

The expansion of industry over the past 25 years has provided factory employment for an ever-increasing number of Chinese. Even in the countryside, small rural workshops are giving the peasants a taste of factory life. In the cities, the eight-hour day and the six-day working week sets the rhythm for most people and the morning and evening rush hours are part of the daily routine. However, it is bicycles and buses that jam the streets and not the private cars found in western cities. Private cars are not sold in China and most vehicles are owned by institutions. It will be a long time before China is rich enough to produce cars for the ordinary consumer.

Because of the wide range of size and purpose, there are inevitably many variations in the structure and operation of China's factories. A small handicraft workshop producing bamboo matting from local resources is much more independent and simply managed than a large machine tool plant producing sophisticated equipment according to the state plan. As a general principle, the larger the factory, the more important its output, the more it relies on expensive modern techniques and the more it uses scarce resources, then the more likely it is to come under close government supervision. The management of such an enterprise has little room to manoeuvre outside the limits set by the authorities. By contrast, small units producing consumer goods from widely available resources and with lower levels of capital investment have much greater independence. The managers of a shoe factory can draw up their own plans for product quality and design, after consultation with their customers. They can also use a proportion of factory profits to invest as they see fit.

Although five-year plans are still used, they are now much less comprehensive. Apart from specific projects, they are usually general outlines which can be revised according to the situation. In practice, the more important plans are those drawn up annually

32 *A factory revolutionary committee at work*

between upper and lower levels of control. Usually the central government in Peking puts forward proposals for resource allocation and production to the provinces. These then consider the suggestions in the light of their capabilities and needs. If necessary, they put forward amendments for incorporation in the final plan. Thereafter the details are settled by negotiations between provincial and municipal agencies and factory management. It is here that most questions about who produces what and who supplies whom are decided.

Within a factory, the two most important bodies are the Party committee and the revolutionary committee. The Party makes all the key decisions, and the actual administration is carried out by the revolutionary committee. The latter's members are Party cadres, managerial and technical staff, and workers' representatives. Committees like these were a major innovation of the Cultural Revolution. They combine political and administrative work, and they also ensure closer contact between management and workforce. Depending on the complexity of the factory, they have offices for such things as production, personnel, planning and statistics, research, welfare and records. An extremely large factory may even have revolutionary committees at workshop level. The workforce itself is divided into workshops and produc-

97

tion squads, each of which elects its own leader to look after job allocation, materials and tools, safety and so forth. In most factories, some attempt is made to involve ordinary workers in technical specialisation either through training courses or through participation in problem solving and design work.

Despite annual fluctuations, a rapid pace of industrial growth was achieved over the years from 1952 to 1972. Real wages have also risen. China's workers have therefore achieved a better standard of living which is reflected in increased consumption of such things as bicycles, wristwatches, radios and better quality clothing. Wages are paid monthly and no tax or welfare payments are deducted from the stated rates. At present there are eight wage grades for industrial workers ranging from around 35 *yuan* per month (roughly £7.70) for apprentices to 100 *yuan* or more for skilled veterans (£21.50). Cadres and technicians have separate grades which rise higher than those of the ordinary labourer. There are also regional differences to match variations in the cost of living, and slight differences between different branches of industry. The average wage in most factories is usually stated to be from 50 to 60 *yuan* a month. Men and women are paid the same rates. Established workers receive full medical insurance and their family is covered for half of all medical expenses. They also get pension rights of around 80 per cent of their final salary. Men

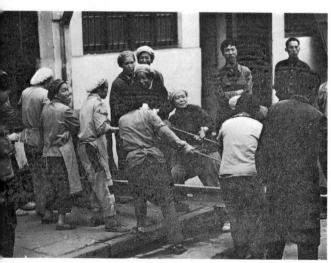

33 *As part of the policy of 'walking on two legs' labour is used as much as possible*

retire at 60 and women at 55.

Until the Cultural Revolution, temporary and contract workers did not receive the same treatment. Their wage rates were lower than the established workers and large numbers of them were paid on a piece-work basis. They were not entitled to any benefits, and after they had finished their contracted employment, they simply transferred to another job or returned to the countryside where most of them came from. Factory managers used them as a cheaper form of labour than established workers. This system received a great deal of criticism during the Cultural Revolution. Reforms were promised though there was no clear statement of what was intended and by 1974 no official announcements had been made.

In the eyes of most Chinese, a factory means much more than a job and a pay packet. A large plant with its own houses and shops forms a very close-knit community. Even a small enterprise with no special facilities dominates the lives of its employees. It is the centre of their official and political life. A worker who is a Party member belongs to the Party organisation within his factory. Political study for everyone is carried out during the factory day. The work card issued by the place of employment is an important means of social identification. Ration coupons, travel permits and even library tickets are obtained through one's unit. The factory also provides for recreational and social activities, ranging from sports teams and reading rooms to cinemas and clubs. A Chinese worker would therefore identify much more closely with his place of work than a worker in most western countries.

Glimpses of Industry at Work

The Nanking Fertilizer Plant is a large-scale enterprise producing over a million tons of phosphate and nitrogenous fertilizers every year. It stands on the north side of the Yangtze River, about an hour's drive from the city of Nanking. Altogether it employs some 12,000 people, who live with their 48,000 dependents in a residential area surrounding the factory complex. The workers not only work together but share the same commercial, cultural and medical services. The factory buildings themselves stretch for several miles along the edge of the river. The oldest parts of the plant were built in 1937 when it employed 1,000 men. By 1949, production had virtually ceased thanks to the shortage of imported raw materials. The state took control of the plant and since that time it has rapidly expanded. Throughout the past 25 years, the plant management has stressed a policy of self-reliance, particularly with regard to developing a wide range of secondary chemical products. In 1961 they successfully introduced a nylon manufacturing plant after the Soviet Union broke a contract promising to help. In 1965 they developed a new granulated fertilizer which saved the cost of importing an expensive process from France.

The Plant is directly subordinate to the Kiangsu Province authorities who make all the final decisions on planned output, investment, allocation of raw materials and distribution of production. The management can influence these decisions by making proposals, but it cannot alter them independently. In 1971, the authorities asked the Plant to produce 900,000 tons of fertiliser. After discussions which involved all the Plant's employees, the management suggested that this target should be raised to 1 million tons. Within the Plant, the management can decide how to use the labour, materials and equipment at its disposal to achieve its targets. It can also make small technical and product innovations provided there is no effect on allocated resources. Major changes can only be made with the approval of higher authorities.

Because of its great size, the Plant is divided into two sub-units —the phosphate and nitrogen groups—which have their own accounting system. This kind of division is common in large industrial enterprises. These groups are in turn divided into a total

34 *Embroidery workers at a cooperative produce modern and traditional designs*

of 33 factories, each concerned with one major process. Revolutionary and Party committees are found at all levels down to the workshop. Wage rates are determined by the national grades. The highest workers' monthly wages is 107 *yuan* (£23.00), the average is 55 and the lowest 34. The top wages for managers and technicians are 110 and 120 *yuan* respectively. In 1971, the Plant could use a small percentage of its funds to pay rewards to workers who overfulfilled their production targets or who introduced successful technical innovations. During 1973, material incentives of this kind were criticised and the system may have been discontinued. Factory discipline is maintained through a code of rules and regulations and by assigning individual responsibility for performing work tasks. In addition there is the pervasive social pressure for good conduct which is expressed in all political propaganda.

The Sian Art and Handicraft Factory is an undertaking at the other end of the scale. This is a cooperative which was set up in 1964 with 70 workers. Some were old craftsmen and some had just graduated from art school. Now there are about 230 workers in ten workshops producing a range of wood and lacquer products, many inlaid with polished stones and ivory. Until the Cultural Revolution, most designs were classical in style featuring historical figures, birds and flowers, but since that time, only export goods (60 per cent of the output) have been like that. Products for domestic markets have depicted revolutionary themes.

Since the factory uses expensive imported items such as ivory, red wood and gold powder, the type of product is decided by the municipal planning bureau. The authorities also set the prices for exported goods, allowing a higher rate of profit than for those sold within China. All other matters are decided by the factory revolutionary committee. Until 1966, the factory was owned collectively by the workers and profits were shared out among them after costs and investment funds had been deducted. This practice has now stopped and the workers are simply paid a monthly salary, the highest being 108 *yuan*, the average 45 and the lowest 36. A third of the workers live in factory dormitories but the rest live in houses scattered about the city.

The Managers

Before the Cultural Revolution, China's industrial managers

enjoyed many advantages over the ordinary workers. Their higher incomes combined with things like the use of the factory car and superior factory housing gave them a better standard of living. They were able to turn this to their families' benefit by providing better clothing, food, medical care and educational opportunities. Apart from token spells on the factory floor, their work involved very little physical labour, which many regarded with some of the traditional bureaucrat's contempt for soiling one's hands. According to the Red Guards, many of them assumed superior bureaucratic airs when dealing with ordinary workers. They ignored the political aims of the Party, and stressed regulations and technical expertise. An example of how this influenced factory operation was reported from a Shanghai wristwatch factory:

> . . . the factory leadership established an overly large administrative set-up and made irrational rules and regulations. If a worker wanted to introduce an innovation he had to go through a lot of red tape; five okays were needed before he could start — from the technicians in charge of his workshop and at factory level, from his workshop head, from the head of the technical section, and, finally, from the chief engineer. The machinery was graded: the few imported lathes, Class A, could only be repaired by technicians at factory level; Chinese-made lathes, Class B, could only be repaired by workshop technicians; and only the workers' own produced equipment, Class C, could be repaired by the workers. Once when a worker changed a screw on a new modern lathe, he was called upon by an irate technical department to make a self-criticism.

After the Red Guard denunciations, the revolutionary committees tried to reduce the distinctions between managers and workers and to prevent the managers from using their position to form a privileged group. They set about simplifying administration by transferring managers to labouring jobs and rescinding many rules. They also ensured continuous contact between workers and managers. Workers became members of revolutionary committees with a say in the running of their factories. Managers spent up to a third of their time doing practical work on a system of rotation between different jobs. Factories expanded training schemes to promote workers into technical and managerial posts. And finally, workers retained the right to criticise managerial decisions.

Inevitably, the manager's life is not what it used to be. He no longer wears the best clothing; he shares canteens and other services with his subordinates, and he is regularly seen on the factory floor working alongside the ordinary employees. Party propaganda daily reminds him not to feel superior to others. Nevertheless, his wage advantage has not disappeared and he still carries out his specialist functions.

These trends have been typical of China's factories since 1969. However, the balance between worker participation in management and specialised control of operations is a delicate one. During 1971 and 1972, some reports in the Chinese media argued that the reforms introduced by the revolutionary committees had gone too far. Product quality and managerial efficiency were declining. The call for care was forcibly expressed:

> Specialised management personnel are a backbone force in enterprise management. Particularly in large enterprises it is imperative to guard against the tendency to put undue stress on management by the masses while ignoring management by specialised personnel.

Many factories announced that they had re-established specialised offices and recalled veteran managers to their posts. But this process provoked a further reaction. Criticisms voiced in 1973 said that the return of personnel and the tightening up of the rules for factory discipline had again led back to some of the problems attacked during the Cultural Revolution. Workers were being ignored and bureaucratic procedures reintroduced. Once more the problem of balance came to the fore.

Faced with all these pressures, the outsider may well wonder why China's managers aspire to do their work at all. Don't they have enough economic problems without political ones too? In fact there were reports during the Cultural Revolution that some managers were dispirited by the attacks on their work. On the other hand, China's continued industrial growth suggests that their efficiency and willingness to get on with the job has not declined. Perhaps one reason for this is their commitment to the development of their country. Every manager I have met has shown a clear pride in the success of his factory, and at the same time, he has become used to the idea of change and development.

As he tells the history of his unit, it is evident that scarcely a year has passed since 1949 without some changes taking place. Furthermore, he also considers politics have an important role to play in factory life. But most of these are public reasons, and if he has any secret ambitions for power and status, these are not openly talked about. Whether the managers would have achieved greater efficiency and success under a different political system is impossible to answer. Certainly, China's pursuit of social justice, equality and selflessness give different criteria for judging success from those found in more selfishly competitive systems.

The Worker

China's workers have a very presitigious social position. Being the proletariat, they are looked upon as the exemplary revolutionary class. This is so even though the revolution was built in the countryside on the basis of mass peasant support. Political discussion in China always stresses that the workers lead the peasants. In books, newspapers and on the stage, they are praised for the virtues of industriousness, self-sacrifice and commitment to communism. This theoretical status is reflected in practical ways. Workers' income, standard of living and welfare benefits are better than those of peasants. They participate in the revolutionary committees that run factories, schools, universities and local government. They also form the units of militia that take part in urban police work.

Nevertheless, the Communist Party does not automatically assume that workers are paragons of political virtue. Like everyone else, they attend daily political study classes, half an hour before work and more time during the day. Campaigns are run to encourage them to pay greater attention to industrial discipline or to practise greater economy. During the Cultural Revolution, the trade unions and some of the large workers' Red Guard organisations were accused of paying too much attention to demanding higher salaries and living standards while neglecting politics and broader issues.

Although factory organisation makes a worker's life very different to that found in other countries, the actual physical work is much the same. Daily shifts last eight hours with a one hour rest period halfway through. Overtime is not usual and, if it is worked, there is no extra payment. Wages are paid at fixed monthly rates as described above. Until 1966, a variety of bonus schemes were used to raise production or to induce people to do particularly unattractive work. In one factory I visited in 1965, workers were paid a ration of pork and eggs for working with ammonia. In another, a percentage of all wages was held back and distributed to the most productive. Most of these disappeared after the Red Guards attacked them. However, the idea of using 'reasonable rewards' as an incentive has since reappeared and it is a touchy subject leading to much debate. Apart from the national festivals such as May Day or National Day (1 October), there are no annual holidays. But if a worker is assigned to a post a long way from his family, he is allowed two weeks paid leave a year to go home and visit them. A worker I met on a train returning to his work after such a holiday did not complain. He was hoping to arrange for his family to move to his new place of work and said that the authorities were usually willing to make such arrangements.

Changing jobs from one factory to another is not easy, as there is no free job market and most assignments are made through the labour bureaus. Once a worker gets an established post within an enterprise, it is very unlikely that he will move from it. Contract and temporary workers tend to move around more often but they are offered jobs and do not wander about looking for them. During periods of slack administrative control, factory managers have been able to employ and dismiss contract workers fairly easily, bringing them in from communes that had a surplus of labour. Should a worker wish to change his job for personal reasons, there is no formal machinery for him to do so. When in Peking in 1971, I noticed private advertisements stuck to walls and lamp-posts in which appeals were made for job exchanges. Typically, a worker in a provincial town stated that he needed to come to Peking for family reasons. He had permission from his factory to move, provided he could find someone to take his place. He was therefore appealing for someone in Peking who might like to swop jobs.

Politically active workers belong to the Communist Party. Communist Youth League and the revolutionary committees within their factories. But nearly all of them belong to trade unions. These are organised on a factory and an industry basis rather than by separate trades, and they are firmly controlled by the Party, During the Cultural Revolution, they were eclipsed by workers' congresses after being accused of political errors, but they have since reappeared. Their main task is to organise political discussion and study. They also act as a channel for expressing workers' opinions to managers and explaining managers' policies to workers. In large factories, the unions provide technical and administrative training, thus forming another avenue of advancement from the factory floor. Outside the factory, the unions help organise educational and recreational activities. Some of them even have sanatoria where the injured and ill can rest and recuperate. In these various ways, the unions play an important role in improving the skills of the workforce and giving them political education. In a situation where many new workers are drawn in from rural areas and have little experience of industrial life, this role is a way of building up the working class and binding them into a new way of life. The unions do not represent the interests of the workers in conflict with the employers but are a means of cooperation between the two.

At Home

The most obvious result of the Communist Party's industrial policies over the past 25 years has been the rapid growth of urban population. Between 1953 and 1959, the number of people living in cities rose from 77 million to an estimated 115 million. Thereafter the rate of increase declined in tune with the policy of sending men and resources down to the countryside, but by 1966 the total had reached around 130 million. This growth in the number of people living in urban areas has put great pressure on the provision of new homes and services. Most cities now have extensive areas of austere but practical apartment houses and are building more. They have also expanded their services with new schools, hospitals, shops, running water, sewers, bus routes and recreational

35 *The Cao Yang Workers' Settlement*

36 *Mrs Gu's kitchen*

facilities. Even so, supply has a hard job keeping up with demand, and there are still areas of old housing lacking basic amenities such as running water and good sanitation.

Much of the new development is planned in integrated housing estates. An example of this is the Cao Yang Workers' Settlement in the northwest suburbs of Shanghai. This estate belongs to the Shanghai Housing Bureau which began to build it in 1951. At first it had a population of 1,200 households with a total of 5,000 family members. By 1971, it had expanded to 15,000 households and 68,000 people. Nearly all the inhabitants are active or retired industrial workers, and most of them have been rehoused from slums. As it has grown, the settlement has set up eight districts, each with its own caretaker and maintenance office to look after general upkeep and repairs. Daily needs are served by the general store, vegetable market and small clinic within each district. The settlement as a whole has a department store, a bank, a post office and a larger clinic to meet more important demands. Serious illnesses are treated at the nearby municipal hospital. The education of the settlement's 35,000 children is in the hands of its

7 secondary schools, 14 primaries, and 13 nurseries and kinder-gartens. When the inhabitants want to relax, there are gardens, a swimming pool, a cinema and a cultural centre.

One resident, a retired silk worker called Gu Zhao-yi enter-tained me to lunch in her home and talked about her life on the estate. She has lived there since 1952. She said that new housing is given to people in need, provided they are politically correct and hard working. She and her husband, who is also retired, have one room and a toilet. They share a kitchen with two other families. Until her son left school and went to work, he also lived in the home. He then moved into the factory dormitory. Now he is married and has his own home on the estate. Mrs Gu's room is on the ground floor of a three-storey block. Her furniture consists of a bed, a chest of drawers, a large cupboard, two tables, some mirrors, and many chests and suitcases. There is no carpet on the bare concrete floor. Although there is nothing luxurious about it, Gu Zhao-yi was proud of her home and the advances it represents over the poverty that once faced most of China's workers.

Both Gu and her husband draw a pension of 40 *yuan* (£8.75) per month and their monthly rent is 3.10 *yuan* plus 1.00 *yuan* for electricity and 0.70 *yuan* for water. Mrs Gu's daily routine is like that of many of her neighbours and other housewives. She gets up at 6.00 a.m., has breakfast and tidies up. Then she does her shopping. Since everyone eats fresh food, and pre-packed or tinned food is expensive, a trip to the market is made by most families early in the day. Lunch is usually eaten around 10.00 a.m. Sometimes they have fish or meat but more often they have vegetables. In the afternoons, Mrs Gu goes to meetings as she is a member of the local residents' committee (see below). When she is not busy, she catches the bus into town to do some shopping or visit a friend. She is also very active in community affairs generally, looking after children for working parents or going shopping for those who can't manage it. In most Chinese cities, old folk do jobs like these and remain important members of society.

Altogether, Shanghai had built 45 housing estates like Cao Yang by 1973. Most large cities have similar projects. In addition, some housing estates are built by or for a large industrial enter-prise. The Nanking Fertilizer Plant is an example. Housing on these estates is reserved for the workers in the related factories.

Outside of the estates, people either live in their own or rented accommodation. The local authority fixes rents in private housing.

While wages have tended to rise over the past 25 years, prices have on the whole remained stable and in some cases even dropped. This has given city dwellers a strong feeling of economic security. All prices are subject to firm government control, and those items that are in scarce supply are rationed. This was true of many goods during the economic crisis of the early 1960s, but the steady recovery of the economy has eliminated most of the rationing restrictions imposed at that time. At present, the two major items that are still rationed are grain and cotton. Every member of a household is issued with coupons to cover his allowance. The grain ration varies according to an individuals' work but is usually between 35 and 50 *jin* (17½–25 kilos) per month. The

37 *The fish market at Cao Yang*

annual cotton ration depends on the harvest and is changed every year. In 1965 in Sian, it was 25 feet per head. In 1971, Mrs Gu and her husband each got 20 feet.

The following list of prices noted at Cao Yang in 1971 will give some idea of what a Chinese worker can get for his average wage of 50 *yuan* a month.

	Price in Yuan (1 *yuan* = £0.22)	
Fresh eggs	0.85	per *jin* (½ kilo)
Chinese sausage	2.76	,,
Salt pork	0.98–1.02	,,
Duck	0.80	,,
Chicken	0.90–1.50	each
Carp	0.40–0.53	per *jin*
Vegetables	0.02–0.06	,,
Apples	0.45–0.60	,,
Rice (best quality)	0.164	,,
Beer	0.50	per litre
Cloth caps	1.00–2.40	each
Cloth shoes	1.50	per pair
Tennis shoes	2.65–4.95	per pair (depending on size and quality)
Porcelain rice bowls	0.15–0.41	each
Transistor radios	40.00	each
Bicycles	90.00–110.00	each

Most families find it easy to meet their basic food and clothing expenses, though those with many children and one wage earner have little left over. People with few dependents can save quite a

38 *The Dong Feng Market in Peking*

39 *A Shanghai delicatessen*

lot, and even pensioners like Mrs Gu find themselves fairly well off. Nevertheless, very few families waste anything. Wrapping paper, string and empty bottles are carefully saved and re-used. Clothes are patched and worn until they have no life left. Although everyone tries to have a best suit of clothes, fashions don't change and there is no pressure to keep up with one's neighbour or continually seek after something new. Advertising in the way it exists in western countries is completely unknown. The luxuries most eagerly sought after by all are bicycles, radios, watches, cameras and sewing machines. Rather more everyday treats are sweets, ice-cream and a meal out. Items such as televisions and fridges are only produced in small numbers. They are much too expensive for individuals and are usually bought by institutions.

As a whole, family life in China is very open and friendly. Families don't stick to themselves behind closed doors but tend to live very closely with their neighbours. In most houses, doors and windows are left open to the streets and the passer-by is always aware of family life going on around him. As soon as winter is over, people move out into courtyards or alleyways, eating, relaxing or doing their chores while chatting to their neighbours in the open air. During the hottest months of the year some families even move their beds outside. The streets are thus always full of bustle and life. Only in areas where the houses face inwards to the courtyards inside, is the foreign visitor unaware of the domestic scene.

Local Government at the Grass Roots

Much of the work of city government such as traffic control, public health, population records and licencing is carried out within municipal and district offices. But at the lowest level of administration, the neighbourhood, the man in the street is actively involved in the running of his city. Peking, for example, has nine districts each of which is divided into neighbourhoods. Fengsheng Neighbourhood is one of nine in the West City District. It has an area of 1·5 square kilometers with 2 main streets and 132 side streets. There are 14,150 households and a total population of nearly 53,000. At the head of Fengsheng Neighbourhood is a revolutionary committee which is elected by the residents and approved by the higher authorities. Under the leadership of the local Communist Party committee, the revolutionary committee carries out the basic administration of the area. Apart from government cadres, who are really assigned rather than elected, the majority of committee members are local residents and workers. Fengsheng's committee has 27 members, 10 of whom are government cadres.

Neighbourhood revolutionary committees control the work of

40 *A bicycle park in Peking, a reflection of growing prosperity*

subordinate bodies called residents' committees. Fengsheng has 25 of these, each representing 400–800 households with an average total of about 2,000 people. Residents' committees are not formal units of government but are informal groups set up by local residents to liaise with and implement the policies of the neighbourhood. Each of them is headed by 15–25 people, locally elected, who serve without pay. Usually each member of a neighbourhood revolutionary committee takes several residents' committees under his wing. For activities such as political study and discussion, the residents' committees organise the households into groups that give 50–60 housewives and retired folk. From the point of view of the Party, this work is very important since it provides one of the chief contacts between people who don't go out to work and the political life of the country. In practice, the members of the neighbourhood revolutionary committee draw up the points to be discussed which are then passed on to the members of the residents' committees who organize the meetings of the small groups. In Fengsheng, these meetings are held 2 or 3 times a week from 8 to 10 in the morning. All members of the neighbourhood revolutionary committee and the residents' committees help lead the discussions. New policies are explained and objections or suggestions raised. In this way, the local government is always well aware of the mood of the people under its control.

Most neighbourhoods run a small number of factories and workshops. These are collectively owned and they are set up in response to local needs or as a part of municipal plans. Fengsheng has seven of these, producing car springs, insulating materials, rubber goods, adults' and children's clothing, metalwork and

41 *A Peking radio factory which has developed from a small unit set up by a neighbourhood and staffed by housewives*

cardboard boxes. There is also an embroidery workshop, though most of the work is done by women in their own homes. All the products are either sold on the market or supplied to nearby factories. Enterprises like these are built and equipped as cheaply as possible, with modern machinery only used where essential. Between 80 and 90 per cent of the staff are women who live locally. Factory income is used to pay wages, provide welfare benefits and support further investment. The Communist Party believes that these undertakings mobilise otherwise unused labour and resources, and are flexible enough to fill gaps not catered for in the state plan.

Neighbourhood revolutionary committees also run nurseries and kindergartens, restaurants, and service shops to do household jobs such as tailoring, mending and washing. Many of these services are intended to help women who want to go out to work. Sometimes there are small clinics where orderlies handle common illnesses and minor injuries. Such clinics form loose links with the municipal hospital services.

The physical maintenance of a neighbourhood area is in the hands of a housing management committee which arranges for people to move in and out of property, renovates old houses and looks after repairs of electricity, water and drains. The neighbourhood revolutionary committee can also negotiate with the higher authorities for extra services such as more taps and drains, or more telephones. In all this work there is a conscious effort to promote the spirit of community service and

42 *Licensed street sellers are still allowed and the ice-lolly trade is popular in the hot climate*

participation.

Crime and Punishment

A variety of formal and informal institutions maintain law and order in Chinese cities. As might be expected, the neighbourhood revolutionary committees, by penetrating deeply into the community, ensure that everyone is to an extent aware of the behaviour expected of him. Criminal tendencies or political deviations can thus be spotted and dealt with in small discussion groups before they give rise to any formal action. Most of the time, this type of social pressure is fairly good-natured. Few people give the impression of always looking over their shoulder in fear of being criticized. Only during political campaigns does it become more insistent.

Encouragement towards good conduct is also found in the media, and in literature, the cinema and the theatre. Countless stories tell about people who find something, go to endless pains to return it to the owner, and refuse to be rewarded. Others describe how vigilant citizens resist temptations to do wrong and eventually bring criminals to justice.

Although reality often falls short of the ideal and everyone takes care to lock their belongings up, most reports suggest there is no large-scale criminal activity in China. During the Cultural Revolution, when social order broke down, large cities experienced some hooliganism, theft and violent crime. Some Red Guard papers had reports of rape and murder. However, the Army firmly suppressed these trends during 1968, sometimes by public trials and executions. Subsequently there has been a return to the stress on honesty and good moral conduct that was characteristic of the years before 1966. The contrast between the corruption of China before 1949 and the moral tenour of life there today, is something that forcefully strikes visitors who have seen both.

Police work in cities is handled by the officers of the public security bureaus. Their work consists of the prevention of crime, the investigation and arrest of criminals, and duties such as traffic control and the issuing of travel and residence permits. In addition, the fire-brigade is a semi-independent department within the same organisation. Usually there is a police station at neighbourhood level and it works closely with the local revolutionary committee in administering civil affairs. The area is divided into 'beats' roughly the size of the residents' committee units, and the policeman ideally forms close relations with the local people so as to keep in touch with what is going on and to deal with problems before they get difficult. Criticisms voiced during the Cultural Revolution suggested that many policemen were far from the friendly figure on the beat they were supposed to be. In most cities, the public security bureaus were strongly criticised and have since been reformed. In 1973 armed units of the workers' militia forces became active in police work, patrolling the streets and dealing with any problems. Since these units are composed of ordinary citizens, albeit the more politically active ones, this arrangement now puts a good deal of responsibility for crime prevention outside the formal police network.

Although the public security bureaus rely heavily on political and social pressure to do their work, they also have a number of coercive weapons. Serious crime such as murder can lead to capital punishment. Minor offences might result in supervision of the individual concerned, more or less like probation in Britain. In between are a variety of forms of imprisonment, ranging from long-term work in a labour camp in a remote area to a short spell in a local camp. In these cases, the emphasis is on reform through labour and political study. Individuals contemplating crime or active political opposition to the Communist Party are aware that they face these sanctions. However, as far as possible, police work in China puts prevention before punishment.

When civil disputes arise such as a quarrel over ownership or a divorce, every effort is made to deal with them before they go to litigation. The idea of informal mediation between conflicting parties has a long history in Chinese civilisation and it continues today as one of the duties of neighbourhood committees. Should agreement not be reached at this level, the problem can be presented to a formally established mediation committee which attempts to solve the case. Only if all these efforts fail, do the litigents finally go to court to obtain a judgement.

Boy meets Girl

Many visitors to China report that it is a drab and puritan society, where even holding hands in public is frowned upon, let alone any more permissive conduct. They point to the lack of feminine

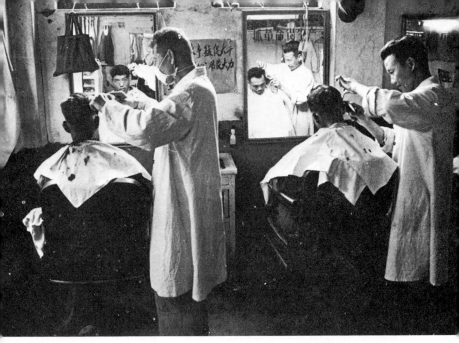

43 *Good barbers stand in high regard and since long hair is frowned upon they do a brisk trade*

fashions and the dull, unflattering clothes the women wear as proof of an oppressive attitude towards sex. A search of contemporary short stories and newspaper reports also shows an emphasis on political and moral relationships between men and women. Romance is rarely mentioned and literary critics argue that too much of it reflects a selfish and degenerate approach to life. At best, the heroine's love for her hero is shown through her admiration for his fine political qualities. It is no surprise that China has gained something of a reputation as a rather prudish country.

Yet, this initial reaction is misleading in many ways. A Chinese looking at British society would be amazed at the amount of time and energy devoted to what he would consider the trivial side of sexual relations. He would see the romance of the love story or the pop song as self-centred and superficial. Make-up, special hairstyles and fashion clothes would seem unnecessary, artificial devices. Instead the Chinese attitude towards sex is much more straightforward. They stress the naturalness of relationships and do not endow them with the special significance they are given in many western countries. The prostitution, polygamy and other liberal practices of the past have been suppressed. But the puritanism is more that of reserve than oppression. The visitor who stays long enough soon realises that plain clothes do not kill sex appeal but transfer it to a person's gestures, mannerisms and personality.

By far the most important change in relationships between men and women has come from the drive for female emancipation. Despite the inertia of tradition, women are becoming the social equals of men in all ways. However, very few girls would take the initiative in dating a boy. This would be seen as highly immoral. In fact most approaches are made by the young man, usually through a mutual friend who helps arrange a meeting. In the towns, educated young people tend to be a bit straight-laced about these things, but in the countryside the approach is much more light-hearted. Many marriages are still arranged by parents but it is now the custom for the young couple to be consulted and to agree before any commitments are made. Pre-marital sexual relations are frowned upon, if discovered. Nevertheless, mistakes are made and, if a girl gets pregnant, abortions are readily available. Most Chinese will tell you that such behaviour is very rare.

Traditionally, people married when young. Now, the Communist Party exerts great pressure to persuade couples to get married in their late twenties. Propaganda stresses the greater ease for single people to devote all their energies to their work and the advantages of small families to women who have fewer fertile years in which to bear children. In practice, many people still feel they would like to marry when young, and during the Cultural Revolution when the Red Guards travelled freely around the country, lots of young couples married. Zhou En-lai is reported as saying that their efforts even increased the national birth rate.

Official statements claim that prostitution has now disappeared and everyone will confirm that this is so. The structure of Chinese society makes it difficult to imagine how it could go undetected for long.

Time Out

As much of this book has shown, political and social activity plays an important part in the life of most Chinese. There is also great pressure to work hard for the economic development of the country. However, it would be wrong for the reader to conclude that all is politics and work, and that there is little room for gaiety and

44 *Amateur musicians practise in a park*

relaxation. Outside of working hours and on his day off, the average citizen finds many ways to relax and enjoy himself.

The lack of television and other commercial amusements in the home means that most families make their own entertainment. Card games are popular and so are board games like chess—both the kind we know in the west and China's own ancient form. Usually children are indulged and sit up late to join in the fun. In hot weather, families sit out in courtyards or in the streets and gossip with their neighbours while enjoying the cool of the evening. Children play a variety of street games, many similar to those of Europe including skipping, hopscotch and marbles. Singing, acting and music are also much liked, though most of this is done in amateur groups associated with the factory or other units.

Sport is extremely popular, with table-tennis and basketball heading the list. On almost every patch of spare ground, groups of people can be seen practising one or the other. Swimming has also gained much support, particularly since Mao's famous swim down the Yangtze in 1966. Generally the emphasis is on

45 *Fruitstall at teashop at the Summer Palace in Peking*

participation. There are no large-scale leagues or tournaments with regular competitions. However, when special matches between factories or provinces are arranged, they are enthusiastically attended. For the less energetic, some of the traditional forms of exercise such as Chinese shadow boxing are also very popular. Early in the morning, parks and gardens are full of men and women practising this graceful and relaxing skill, completely absorbed in what they are doing and oblivious of the scene around them. Even the appearance of a strangely dressed foreigner with a retinue of interested observers will not distract them from their routine.

For a special outing, the family has a variety of choices. A trip to the zoo or local park is always popular. In most such places, there is a boating pond or a tea pavilion where a few cents will buy some green tea and some melon seeds to chew. Most cities have an old temple or palace now transformed into a museum or park where citizens can relax in traditional surroundings. In Soochow, for example, there are many famous old aristocratic gardens open to the public, where the careful balance between courtyard, pond, pavilion and garden forms a delightful and constantly changing pattern as one walks around. Just outside Loyang lie the Buddhist grottoes at the gorge of Longmen where

46 *The Buddhist Grottoes at Longmen remind the Chinese of their cultural heritage as well as provide a place to go on a day off*

47 *A typical scene in a newly-built restaurant*

families spend the day picnicking beside the river and admiring the striking carvings on the rock faces.

In the evening, a family might choose to go out to one of the many restaurants found about their city. Usually they are not restricted to a choice of meals cooked in the style of their own province, in fact most large cities have a variety of restaurants specialising in the cuisines of other parts of the country. Shanghai and Peking even have a few places where western-style food is served. Alternatively, the family might go to the cinema or to the local operatic drama, though the shows are always well booked and tickets are not easy to get. Drinking and gambling are officially disapproved of and there are no special clubs or premises where people can indulge. Compared with European cities, night life ends very early and by ten o'clock most families are at home and ready for bed.

Finally there are the traditional and modern festivals. At New Year, the special rice dumplings and other foods are prepared, lucky sayings are pasted on the walls, and small presents are given. At Spring Festival, the family graves are swept and, a new tradition, revolutionary martyrs are commemorated. The Autumn Moon Festival is the time to eat the rich moon cakes stuffed with dates and nuts, and you must make a point of admiring the new moon. On National Day, the founding of the People's Republic is celebrated with colourful parades, firework shows, special dinners and evening entertainments. Traditions and spectacles like these are things that the Chinese look forward to and which add sparkle to their daily lives.

5
Education and Culture

If you ask a Chinese Communist about the role of education and culture in society, he will tell you that they are parts of the superstructure, the outgrowth of the economic base. He will define the values they embody, the goals they set, and the ways in which they are organised in terms of the economic structure of his country. He will also insist that all education and culture reflects the social class to which it belongs. However, his view is not a mechanical one which says that social change must come first and changes in schools and in the arts will follow automatically. The Chinese believe that conscious revolution in education and the arts is an important way of helping the new society develop from the old. Education must strive to create the ideal man, and the arts must reflect his attributes. The individual must work to remould his outlook to match the new ideas. When he learns to read and write or when he paints a picture, he should do so not for his own ambition or simply for relaxation but in order to serve the revolution.

The Background of Educational Reform
The basic purpose of education in China is to promote the growth of a modern communist society. To achieve this end, it must fulfil three main functions. It must teach prescribed skills and knowledge such as reading, writing, arithmetic, geography, and science; it must inculcate loyalties to China, to the policies of the Party and Mao, and to Marxism; and it must encourage behaviour which is industrious, honest, and aimed at the collective good. The schools are not the only bodies in China to do these things, but because of their key formative role they are one of the most

122

important. However, the Chinese have faced many problems in building a system to match their needs. The influence of tradition, the schools inherited in 1949, and the problems of economic development have all placed obstacles in their way.

A major legacy of tradition has been the strong emphasis on moral education. Academic and moral learning have always been closely united and the modern domination of the schools by moral and political education is not an innovation. What is new is the nature of the morality taught. The old Confucian cannons have given way to new Marxist beliefs.

Another feature of the past was the close association between education, social status and political power. Only the educated were eligible to become members of the ruling official class. And, with few exceptions, it was only the rich who could afford the time and money to be educated. The Communists have constantly criticised this unity of schooling, class and power. They insist that their new schools should guard against the growth of a privileged elite. Within the classroom, traditional methods in old China were very authoritarian, teachers demanded great respect and discipline. Much of school life consisted of rote learning and the repetitition of orthodoxy. Despite the changes that have been going on throughout this century, many of these traditional attitudes towards the relationship between education and social status and the role of the teacher have persisted to influence Chinese schools today.

The educational structure the Communists inherited in 1949 owed much of its origin to the work of missionaries and other foreigners during the previous hundred years. They had opened schools, colleges and universities—all modelled on western lines. Many of these remained in independent existence right up until 1949. Others had been set up by the Imperial Government in 1905 as part of its limited attempts to modernise the country. It introduced a school system copied from the Japanese who had in turn taken it from the French. Once the Republic was set up in 1911, further modification and experiment led to the adoption by 1922 of a system based on the American pattern. These schools, their courses and much of their teaching material were directly copied from abroad with the Nationalist government firmly controlling the curricula and the political content. However, although this system marked an immense break with the past, it failed to affect the great bulk of the people. Teachers and equipment were scarce and few could afford the fees to go through all the stages. The political situation was never stable enough for the schools to be consolidated. They only functioned in the cities, and much of what was taught was alien to the peasant masses. By the late 1940s, government statistics recorded that less than five per cent of the population of over 500 million was receiving full-time education.

The lack of schools and colleges was only a symptom of China's general economic backwardness. After 1949, tremendous efforts were needed to expand the school system, not only to provide places for the tens of millions of children who had never had the chance to go to school but also to produce the trained personnel to undertake the work of modernisation. Yet the resources were all lacking. There were neither teachers, nor equipment, nor the funds to supply them quickly. Moreover, education had to compete with the equally pressing claims of agriculture, industry, medical welfare and so forth. It was vital to avoid waste and ensure that the new schools closely matched priorities. Given the economic situation, the Chinese had to decide, for example, whether they wanted to educate large numbers of mechanics cheaply or whether they needed a smaller number of engineers trained at a higher cost, a decision which has not been easy to make. Sometimes concentration on introducing universal basic education has resulted in rapid growth at the expense of quality. Again, they have not always been able to forecast accurately the demand for different kinds of specialists or to ensure that they were trained in the right way. A story that circulated during the Cultural Revolution told of a graduate in railway bridge design who couldn't handle other railway design problems or other types of bridges. While this story may have been exaggerated, it does illustrate the difficulties of judgement facing China's educational planners.

Policies and Problems

Since 1949, educational policy in China has been influenced by two very different approaches. The mainstream centred on a strong, centralised structure copied from the Soviet Union and built on the foundations of the existing schools. The alternative stressed decentralisation and flexibility. It drew from the experience of the wartime guerrilla base areas, where the Communists were cut off from the school system and were forced to resort to other experiments. Sometimes the two approaches have coexisted side by side and at other times there has been conflict. The Cultural Revolution brought about a major confrontation.

Until 1966, the Soviet model was represented in China by a full-time system of schools, institutes and universities, all under the control of the Ministries of Education and Higher Education, both of which merged into one for the period 1958 to 1964. These central authorities had ultimate responsibility for all schools and took the general decisions on such things as organisation, courses and finance. A body of rules and regulations determined all aspects of school life and the conditions of the school environment.

Primary school lasted from 7 to 12, junior secondary school from 13 to 15 and senior secondary from 15 to 18. Most university courses lasted four years. The great majority of secondary schools were 'general secondary schools' giving a standard academic education. A small number were vocational schools training pupils in technical skills, and another small group trained teachers to work in the first years of primary school. In addition to the universities, a large number of specialist institutes were set up on the Soviet pattern. These concentrated on one subject or a group of related subjects, and could only produce graduates in that limited field. At each level there was a comprehensive range of courses, using teaching materials written under central guidance. Much of this was directly translated from Soviet textbooks. A great deal of emphasis was given to scientific and technical subjects, and there was a strong inclination towards the theoretical and academic rather than the practical.

Although limited resources made it inevitable that schools often had to make do with old or unsuitable buildings and poor equipment, the ideal school required a good deal of investment. This led to a bias towards urban areas, where there was a great enough concentration of population to justify the expense. In rural areas, where transport was poor and schools fewer, many were built as boarding schools with their own dormitories and canteens.

Despite considerable investment and growth at the primary level, the provision of places in this full-time system was never able to meet demand. According to official figures, the number of

48 *Lunchtime at the kindergarten. Ravioli soup and oil cakes*

pupils enrolled in primary schools rose from 24 million in 1949 to 90 million in 1959. This represented a rise of from less than 30 per cent to over 80 per cent of eligible children attending school. But in the same period enrolment at secondary level only rose from 2 million to about 10 million. Since in 1953 alone there were around 75 million teenagers of secondary school age, the attendance was far from what it could have been. Figures like these underline the extent to which primary education has been the only education available to most Chinese. An important result of this shortage of secondary school places was that only the most able were selected for secondary school education, and this selection was based on successful completion of the primary course and a pass in the school entrance examinations. Similar tests were faced at university level. Many teachers and schools concentrated on getting good examination results and built up reputations for getting passes. They attracted bright pupils and could raise the standards for their own intake. During the early 1960s, the existence of this network of successful schools was officially recognised when the government decided to rationalise expenditure. It chose a number of them throughout the country for special treatment. Instead of limited resources being widely spread, investment was concentrated in them so as to ensure that they, at least, came up to the highest standards, thus creating a privileged hierarchy within the educational system.

This privilege was strengthened by the fact that education was not free. Although the average tuition fees were not high, amounting to 5 or 6 *yuan* per year, they were not negligible to a worker earning 50 or 60 *yuan* a month, particularly if he had several children to pay for. Moreover, the rate was not standard and the better schools tended to charge more. Textbooks and stationery also had to be bought. One boarding kindergarten I visited in the city of Chengchow in 1966 charged 13.50 *yuan* per month for each child. A similar institution in Peking charged 25 *yuan*. Both were extremely well equipped with a fully trained staff and even a school doctor. In some secondary schools tuition fees could be as much as 20 *yuan* per year and the boarding charges from 10 to 15 *yuan* per month. There were no fees at university, and scholarships were given to cover living costs. But pocket money still had to be found. In 1956, one Chinese newspaper estimated that to keep a child at school cost 120 *yuan* per year. Other estimates put the cost even higher. The combination of high educational standards, high fees and a shortage of school places tended to favour the richer elements of society and especially those living in cities.

Despite occasional attempts to introduce greater flexibility into school regulations to match the needs of different localities and more political study and practical work to balance academic training, this full-time school system resisted modification. It remained committed to an ideal of academic and professional expertise based on a closely controlled, standardised, and meticulous approach. Its supporters were confident that it best served the requirements of a modern society, supplying planned amounts of trained manpower and giving a proportion of the population some access to prescribed standards of learning.

After 1966, the Red Guards sharply attacked this system. They blamed Liu Shao-qi and his associates for its defects. The most obvious target was its inherent urban bias. They quoted examples to illustrate the growing inequalities between town and countryside. Deng County in Shantung Province reported that in 1965 only 40 per cent of all the children in the county attended school. In 1968, a Heilungkiang commune said that in 54 poor peasant families surveyed there were 30 young people aged between 18 and 20 who were illiterate. Apart from the lack of schools, many other factors militated against the peasant child. The cost of education was particularly important. For peasant families with incomes rarely above 400 *yuan* per year, the prospect of paying out over 100 to get the best education for just one child was not at all realistic. Even a worker could ill afford it. But the problem was accentuated in the countryside since, unlike the cities, a young child could earn money for his family by working in the fields or on the family plot. Sending a child to school not only meant paying fees but also forgoing his earning potential. As a result increasing numbers of peasant children were withdrawn from school as they grew older and were more able to work on the land. Even now this problem has not been solved. Peasant children can still add to family income and parents are not legally obliged to send their children to school.

Another problem facing the peasants was the standardisation of courses. Because of the wide variation in climate and way of life, no single textbook could cater for everyone. Moreover, the stress on academic learning did not prepare the children for the sort of jobs they had to do on leaving school. The Red Guards complained that the blackboard exercises could not be put to practical use, yet many pupils felt superior to the uneducated. On a commune in Shantung this was described as 'primary school students look down on their own parents, secondary school students look down on the cadres of the production brigade, and college students think themselves too great to stay in the village.'

A further major target for Red Guard criticism was the combination of selective schools and tuition fees. They argued that this was working against the class interests of peasants and workers. Between 1952 and 1958, the proportion of workers' children in higher education only increased from 20 to 36 per cent. The remainder came from families of cadres, intellectuals, and those defined as bourgeois, capitalist and landlord. The highest concentrations of upper-class children tended to be in the better universities studying subjects like music and medicine. According to some reports, the special school system or 'treasure pagoda' as it was nicknamed was increasing the discrimination against children from poor families by recruiting most of their intake from the better-off. In important cities, a number of these well-endowed schools took children almost exclusively from the families of leading cadres. A notorious example was the Number 2 Primary School in Peking where many of China's leaders sent their children. The existence of these schools supported the Red Guards' claim that the school system was producing a new ruling elite. The members of this student elite paid greater attention to their academic studies and passing examinations than to politics. They were more interested in their own careers than in serving the needs of society. It was alleged that when such people were appointed to important posts in the Party, government and management, they ceased to be revolutionaries and began to form a revisionist ruling class. In 1971, a young primary school teacher in Peking told me that as an intellectual she once felt very superior to the masses and didn't think she could learn from them. She was mainly interested in her job and her own comfort. Since the Cultural Revolution, she had learnt to 'serve the people' and not herself and was now prepared to do any kind of work. Whatever the sincerity of such comments, they do show the importance attached to this problem by the Chinese today.

The Alternative

In attacking the Soviet model, the Red Guards were not attempting to deal with the issue of how, with limited resources and a pressing demand for all types of specialists, intensive professional training should be organised. Instead they were more concerned with an egalitarian distribution of educational opportunity, with the social and political content of education, and with forging a closer relationship between schools and the immediate social problems. Their ideal was the educational system that had evolved in wartime Yenan and which all along had offered a challenge to the full-time system.

The war situation before 1949 and the lack of resources in the communist base area had made it impossible to operate a centrally controlled, standardised system. The only alternative had been to decentralise authority and allow complete flexibility to match local conditions. The authorities gave general guidance but the details were left to the man on the spot. The teachers and local peasants made all the decisions about their school and provided their own finance. Many schools were entirely self-supporting, paying their own way and growing their own food. They functioned very informally. There were no age limits and old and young joined whatever classes suited them. Teachers organised classes to meet demand, and related what they taught to production so that the peasants could get immediate benefits. There was no teacher training, and most teachers simply taught the skills they used in daily life. The students were encouraged to learn by doing rather than by rote. The primary aim of these schools was to integrate what they taught and the way they operated with the society around them. The Communist Party found this approach to education popular and successful. The peasants supported it and it served the needs of the time and in addition, was self-reliant and cheap.

After 1949, attention had moved to the full-time system. Only two aspects of the Yenan model lingered on: the mass literacy campaigns, when informal classes were held everywhere to overcome the 90 per cent illiteracy rate; and the spare-time classes for workers, which mainly taught technical skills. The other informal schools soon closed down.

During 'The Great Leap Forward' of 1958 attempts were made to reintroduce the Yenan approach. Mao called for the rapid growth of education more closely related to productive labour and with greater political content. He wanted to unite mental and manual work, theory and practice, in the way it had been done in Yenan. Communes, factories and mines responded by establishing their own 'part-work part-study' schools. The pupils spent half the day studying and half the day working. By 1960 over 30,000 such schools had been set up with around 3 million pupils. The speed of expansion together with poor teaching from people who often had little education themselves meant that, whatever the political and practical gains, academic standards were very low. The most ambitious project was the founding of workers' universities. These were really technical training centres providing short courses in skills required by industry and agriculture. Unlike the students in standard universities, the worker-students spent a great deal of their time working in factories on the sort of job they would be assigned to after graduation.

The collapse of many of the Great Leap policies also led to a cut back in these irregular schools and universities. Most were closed and the rest became seasonal with half the year spent in the classroom and half out at work. This converted them into ordinary schools with less time in which to do the work. The peasants looked down on them, and the original purpose was destroyed. Official policy treated them as a stop-gap which would gradually disappear as the full-time system expanded. That these schools represented an entirely different concept of education was ignored. It was not until the Cultural Revolution that the issue was brought to the surface again. Between 1966 and 1968, with the exception of primary schools, nearly all education stopped while the merits of the two approaches to education were debated. It is only since 1971 that the new pattern of school organisation has begun to emerge and, even so, many of the problems are not yet solved.

Primary Schools

A major result of the Cultural Revolution has been a switch of educational resources from the towns to the poorer rural areas. The target has been to provide primary education for all peasant children. At the same time, greater attention is now being paid to basic, practical education. Academic and theoretical studies have been reduced. Communes have once again established large numbers of part-time schools. Many rural areas now report from 80 to 90 per cent of primary school age children attending school. However, the full-time schools still exist. They have been modified to include more practical work and politics, and the specially selective 'treasure pagoda' system has been abolished, but the quality of urban education is still better than that of the countryside. And although selection procedures have radically changed, specialist training is only available to a limited number of people.

The old six-year primary course is now reduced to five years, and this has been achieved by cutting down on academic courses and by combining subjects where possible. Full-time schools are under the general direction of the cultural and educational bureaus that are part of local government. The irregular, part-time schools are run by production brigades and production teams in the countryside and by neighbourhoods in the towns. In all cases, the emphasis is on frugality of operation and a large degree of self-sufficiency. All schools have a revolutionary committee, whose director has taken over the role formerly played by the headmaster. He is usually a Party cadre and his committee includes teachers, pupils, parents and workers or peasants. Some of the bigger schools also have a militia leader or a soldier. The full committee only meets to make important decisions about the school. The day-to-day administration is left in the hands of a small group of committee members, who control all matters such as the hiring and firing of teachers, student matters, the contents of the syllabus and the supervision of political work. In the full-time schools, much of this must be done in consultation with the local educational authorities. The part-time schools have greater freedom.

The quality of the schools varies considerably. A full-time school in a city often has new buildings with well-lit rooms, workman-like if old-fashioned school desks, good blackboards, and a useful range of modern teaching aids including tape-recorders, film and slide projectors, and general science equipment. There are sports grounds with facilities for various games— especially basketball, table-tennis and volley ball—and special areas where displays can be made of political propaganda, health and welfare information, and the pupils' own literary and artistic efforts. Most such schools have a library, and in few cases these hold several thousand books. Although there is no extravagance—buildings are plain with concrete floors, central heating is rare, and sports grounds are made of beaten earth—most things are functional and efficient. By contrast, a rural part-time school operates in any convenient building, often a converted temple or peasant house. There is no proper equipment and ordinary tables and chairs are used, together with a makeshift blackboard. This is supplemented by the actual implements used on the commune, the farmer's tools or the accountant's abacus. Such things are intended to integrate the school with its community

49 *The abacus is used to teach arithmetic in the primary school*

as much as to make up for deficiencies in other equipment.

The organisation of the school year now varies throughout the country. Full-time urban schools have two terms running from September to January and February to July. In rural areas, this may be further divided into three or four terms with holidays planned to suit the local agricultural calendar. Pupils attend school for six days a week. In the part-time schools, terms are determined according to local conditions. Some schools study for half the day and work for the other half, and others work and study on alternate days. Where the population is scattered, the teachers travel around from hamlet to hamlet so that the school only meets once or twice a week in each place. In other cases, classes are held in the morning, afternoon and evening to cater for different groups of pupils. Most classes in the full-time schools have around 45 children of the same age, but the part-time schools are prepared to take larger numbers and a wider range of ages. Tuition fees do not exist in the irregular schools but apart from the cancellation of excessive charges the 5 or 6 *yuan* fees for the full-time schools remain in force.

School lessons have three main elements, basic learning, political training and manual labour. During the Cultural

jiāo shuǐ　　chú cǎo　　shàng féi
浇　水　　锄　草　　上　肥

xiāo miè chóng hài　　xiāo miè bìng hài
消　灭　虫　害　　消　灭　病　害

50 *A page from a school book. The text reads: 'The people's communes are good. When people are many their strength is great. They put on more fertilizer, hoe the weeds, wipe out pests and fine crops grow'*

rén mín gōng shè hǎo,　rén duō jìn tóu gāo,
人　民　公　社　好，　人　多　劲　头　高，

duō shàng féi　qín chú cǎo
多　上　肥，　勤　锄　草，

xiāo miè bìng chóng hài　zhuāng jià zhǎng de hǎo
消　灭　病　虫　害，　庄　稼　长　得　好。

广———病

长	灭	害	病	消	浇
肥	劲	勤	稼	锄	

Revolution, politics and labour were stressed much more than classroom learning but now the balance has changed and 80 per cent of school time is spent on the latter. Basic learning includes such things as reading, writing, and arithmetic. In the full-time schools the curriculum is fairly comprehensive and might even include a foreign language, whereas the part-time schools have to make do with the resources they have. A typical example of a full-time school is the Chengxian Jie Primary School in Nanking which I visited in 1971. School begins at 8 a.m. and the first half hour is spent studying the works of Mao and discussing current affairs. This is followed by 20 minutes of physical exercises. There are four classes in the morning starting at 8.55 and each lesson lasts 40 minutes with a 10 minute break in between. After lunch there is a rest period, the time allowed being longer in summer than in winter. The two afternoon classes start at 2 p.m. and the pupils go home at 3.35. Each week there are the following number of classes for each subject:

Chinese	10–12
Mathematics	6
Politics	4
Art	2
Physical Training	2
General Knowledge	1

Language study takes up about half of all primary education because of the difficulties of learning the Chinese written system. Instead of using letters, the Chinese use units of meaning called 'characters'. For most purposes a basic vocabulary of 3,000 will do but to read a wide range of books and literature easily and with no reference to a dictionary you need to know about 7,000 of them. Learning characters is a slow process of copying them out and memorising each one. Graduates of primary school are expected to know about 3,000. Because of the time and effort this takes, language lessons are also used to teach other things, particularly politics and good behaviour. The political content centres on writings by Mao and the policies of the Communist Party. Strong patriotism is encouraged as is devotion to Mao and communism. There is criticism of capitalism and support for revolutionary movements throughout the world. Usually each new political development in China adds another theme to the texts studied. Pupils are taught to hate the 'old society' before

1949 and to guard against any enemies who still exist. A lesson in a 1966 textbook for nine year-olds declared:

The Party is My Mother

How happy life is today but I will never forget the tragic days before Liberation.

Then our family ate only breakfast and did not have any afternoon meal. The reactionary government of the Nationalists and landlords didn't care what happened to us and often came to make us pay taxes and rent. Their flunkies, like wolves and tigers, always beat the people with whips. My father couldn't remember how many times he was cruelly beaten. The year I was eight, there was a bad drought in our village, and everyone ate plant stalks and tree bark to satisfy their hunger. In September, my father and mother both starved to death. Tearfully my grandfather sold me to Huang Lao-ba, the landlord, in exchange for money for coffins. He then buried mother and father. Thereafter, my grandfather begged for food and I became a slave to Huang Lao-ba.

Huang Lao-ba simply did not consider me a human being. I worked from early morning to late at night without any rest. Even so he said I loafed on the job. If he wasn't cursing me he was beating me, and very often he gave me nothing to eat. In Winter he gave me only a bundle of rice straw, and I was so cold I shivered. All year long I wore a single ragged dirty gown. My hair grew long but it was not cut. My face grew pale and my flesh melted away until I did not look human at all.

After Liberation, Huang Lao-ba was overthrown and a house and land were distributed to our family. The two of us, grandfather and grandson, were reunited. We took part in a mutual aid team and later in an agricultural producers' cooperative. With the establishment of the people's communes in 1958, our life improved from year to year.

I have often felt that the Party is my mother. If it weren't for the Party, where would today's happiness be? I must work actively and study hard, forever going along with the Party!

The last line of this lesson illustrates the sort of good behaviour encouraged in primary schools. The pupils are called upon to be obedient, self-sacrificing, industrious and honest. Many of the stories they read show them what is meant by doing one's duty and helping the collective. For example, one lesson tells how a child stopped his family's chickens from straying into the commune fields and eating the commune grain. Although this meant the chicken had less good food to eat, it also meant that his family did not prosper at the cost of the collective. Within schools the children have jobs to do like cleaning up the yard or tidying the classroom. These are intended to promote the idea of serving their community. If a child provides a striking example of good behaviour, he may be given special praise and held up as a model for others to copy.

In political lessons, the pupils study communist writings and what the ideas expressed mean for their daily life. They might learn an article by Mao off by heart, and then discuss the relationship between it and the work they would like to do when grown up. However, political ideas also permeate most subjects. In mathematics, for example, problems are set asking the pupils to work out how much the landlords exploited their tenants before 1949, or how many enemy troops were put out of action each day in the war in southeast Asia. In painting lessons, the pupils draw pictures of revolutionary events and symbols. When they sing, they sing songs about building communism. Outside school, children join in all demonstrations and parades. They form small propaganda groups to publicise political ideals and Party policies in their homes and in the surrounding neighbourhood. During a road safety campaign, they will organise patrols at the side of the road, reading out slogans on road sense and

51 *Children at Chengxian Jie Primary school assemble petrol filters*

ideology. In these ways, children are actively involved in the political life of the country and learn the importance of a strong commitment to communist ideas; dissenting attitudes are sharply criticised.

Manual labour is most prominent in the part-time schools. Here, the pupils spend half their time working in the fields or in factory workshops. Although much of their productive labour is valuable to the economy, Party leaders argue that its main aim is educational, since they believe that labour is the source of all knowledge and morality. In the full-time schools, this work is done in small school workshops and by working in factories and communes for short periods of time. At the Chengxian Jie Primary School, the pupils assemble petrol filters for car engines, make other car fittings, and build their own school equipment. They also grow grain and vegetables on small plots of land. Each class spends a few hours in the workshops each week. After the third year, they go in groups to the countryside or to factories to work for one or two weeks at a stretch.

Although examinations were criticised during the Cultural Revolution and are still the subject of debate, many full-time schools do test their pupils to decide on how they should progress through the school. In November 1973, one Peking school reported that each year examinations are set to see how the pupils have advanced. If a pupil fails, he can have a resit before the new school term begins. Failure again in two major subjects such as political study, Chinese or arithmetic, or in one major and two minor subjects might lead to the pupil having to repeat his previous year's studies before promotion to the next grade. Furthermore, each pupil has a report book to take home at the end of the year. The teacher reports on the child's scholastic achievements, his attitude towards study and labour, his behaviour, his ability to mix, and his attitude towards the collective and public property. With older children, the teachers also note how they study for the revolution, and what interest they take in national affairs. Thus the children are not free from academic pressures.

Secondary Schools

As at the primary level, full-time and part-time secondary schools operate side-by-side. However, most of the part-time schools only cater for the junior secondary school level. This is particularly true of rural areas, where the rapid expansion of part-time secondary education has meant that from 60 to 70 per cent of children aged 12 or 13 now attend the first few years. In fact, in many places primary schools have simply added an extra two years of junior secondary education to their courses, rather than communes seeking to set up independent secondary schools.

The role of the examination in the move from primary school to secondary school has now been abolished. Provided a child successfully completes his primary courses, he can move directly to the secondary school which serves his area. In part-time schools even this qualification is unnecessary. But during 1972 and 1973, there was a tendency to renew the emphasis on academic standards as the Cultural Revolution preference for political achievement above scholastic receded into the background. Party committees in Fukien explained this change by arguing that a distinction had to be made between 'necessary cultural assessments, aimed at getting acquainted with a student's achievements under the guidance of the correct political line' and 'using tests as a means of controlling, restricting and oppressing workers, peasants and soldiers'. They also said that this did not mean a return to the old policy of 'putting marks in first place'. They believed that it was still necessary to consider 'political merits and practical experience' as basic qualifications when selecting students. Nevertheless, the defensive tone of these arguments was clear and by the end of 1973 a fresh wave of criticism of examinations was given great publicity throughout the country. The problem of how to assess people for advancement to the higher levels of education still remains a very contentious issue.

The organisation of secondary schools is much the same as that of the primaries. Revolutionary committees are in charge with Party, teacher, worker and student representatives. Politics and manual labour are also stressed as much as academic studies, and there is much experiment to reduce the total number of years of study from six to four or five.

An example of the best of secondary education is the Number 31 Secondary School in Peking. Before 1949, the school had been run by missionaries and the old chapel buildings remain as a meeting hall, though most of the other buildings are new. This school was often quoted in the national press as a model institution before

1966, when 50 to 70 per cent of its pupils regularly went on to university. It is still regarded as a successful school and many foreign visitors are taken to see it. The 12 courses now taught are political study, Chinese, English, mathematics, physics, chemistry, basic agriculture, history, geography, revolutionary art, physical training and hygiene. The school workshops include a car electrical circuit assembly shop, a printed circuit production unit and a workshop for making radio valves. The school day is as follows:

0800 School assembles, study of Mao's works.
0810 First class (each class lasts 50 minutes).
0900 Second class.
0950 Break and a spell of collective exercises in the school yard.
1020 Third class.
1110 Fourth class.
1200 Lunch break.
1400 Fifth class.
1450 Sixth class.
1540 Current affairs discussion groups.
1600 Extracurricular activities including sports, manual labour and political meetings.
1830 School closes.

Most of the children live in the surrounding area and very few are now boarders. However, the school can provide school lunches for those who cannot go home. On average, there is one hour of

52 *A serious reader at Shanghai's Children's Library*

53 *Secondary school pupils play a lunchbreak game of table-tennis while spending a month working at the Shanghai Machine Tool Plant*

homework each night. There are two terms a year with eight to ten weeks holiday altogether. Classes are held six days a week. Usually the pupils spend a month every year working in communes and in factories.

By contrast, rural part-time schools are much more rudimentary. Subjects like physics, chemistry and foreign languages are far beyond their resources. Instead the emphasis is on productive labour and practical skills. Classroom studies are associated with work on the job, and the pupils run experiments on such things as seed selection, the introduction of new crops and other technical problems. While the state will provide some funds for these schools, especially for the salary of any trained teachers, most of the finance must come from the units which run them and from the schools' own production.

Since the Cultural Revolution, the Ministry of Education has not functioned and its work has been done by the State Council Committee for Science and Education. Many of the regulations that were in force before 1966 are now being revised. However, the following rules for secondary school students still give a good idea of the sort of behaviour expected from teenagers in China.

Rules for the Conduct of Secondary School Students
(June 1955)

1. Endeavour to learn; learn to be good in health, good at study, and good in conduct. Prepare to serve the motherland and the people.

2. Respect the national flag. Respect and love the leader of the people.

3. Obey the regulations of the school. Obey the instructions of the principal and the teachers.

4. Arrive at the school punctually and attend the classes punctually. Never be late; never leave the school before time; and never miss a class without reason.

5. When attending school everyday, bring all the textbooks and stationery required. Before the class begins, prepare all the things required for the lesson.

6. During the class assume a correct posture; listen to the lecture attentively; do not talk unless when necessary; do not do anything else besides your classwork. When desiring to leave the classroom, ask the teacher's permission first.

7. Stand up when answering the teacher's questions. Sit down when the teacher permits you. When you want to ask the teacher a question raise your hand first.

8. Perform your private study carefully. Finish your work in all subjects in time.

9. Respect the principal and the teachers. Stand up and salute your teacher when the class begins and again at the end of the class. When you meet the principal or the teachers outside the school you also salute them.

10. Be sincere and friendly with your schoolmates, unite with them and help one another.

11. Respect and love your parents. Love and protect your brothers and sisters. Help the family do the housework.

12. Respect your elders. Respect the aged. Love and protect the children; take care of the sick and infirm; give them your seat on a carriage; give way to them on the road.

13. Be honest, sincere, modest and polite to people. Do not tell a lie. Do not curse people. Do not fight. Do not disturb people's work, study, or sleep.

14. Do not smoke. Do not drink. Do not gamble. Do not take away other people's things without permission. Do not do anything that may be harmful to yourself or to others.

15. Take plenty of exercise and make your body strong. Keep your body, clothes, quarters, and all public places clean and hygienic.

16. Obey public order. Take care of public property.

17. Value and protect the reputation of the class and of the school.
18. Always have your student identity card with you and see that you do not lose it.

Higher Education

Of the small number of young people who eventually graduate from senior secondary school at the age of 16 or 17 very few go directly to college or university. Most of them are assigned to jobs in industry, commerce, agriculture and the army. They can only apply for further education after they have done one or two years' work. As at the secondary school level, the question of selection is the cause of much debate. Immediately after the Cultural Revolution entrance examinations were abolished. Selection was based on five main criteria. First students had to come from the ranks of workers, peasants and soldiers, with only a small proportion from other social groups. Second, they had to have shown a high degree of enthusiasm in studying and applying Mao's works. Third, they had to be about 20 years old and have already spent some years at work. Fourth, they had to have completed at least junior secondary school and have achieved an 'acceptable' educational level. Finally, they had to be in good health. The process of applying for a university place began with the individual asking the unit that employed him to consider his case. This was done by discussion among his workmates and employers. If they approved, the candidate was recommended to the local authorities who in turn examined his case and recommended him to the university. The latter then sent down a recruiting team to consider applicants from a particular area. Thus both recommendation and selection were involved.

However, during the early 1970s, the universities found the quality of the students they were getting did not match the courses they were offering. They had to organise extra preparatory classes and supplementary training. So once again they introduced examinations to test the quality of their applicants, who could choose to sit for one or two subjects depending on the course they intended to follow. The Hupeh Student Enrolment Office, which handles student applications for further education in the province of Hupeh, stated that 'culture tests are to be conducted for those who have been recommended by the masses and who have been successful in political examination, so as to find out their capacity in study and in grasping basic knowledge and analysing and solving problems, and to guarantee that the students have actual cultural standards corresponding to junior secondary education or above'. The Office also pointed out that if, within three months of admittance, a student's qualifications were found to be not good enough, he would be sent back to his unit.

This reversal of policy upset many of the young people who had gone to work in factories and the countryside, hoping to go to university on the basis of their political and practical experience. Many of them found the examinations too difficult since they had not had the chance to do any studying. In June 1973, one of these students, called Zhang Tie-sheng, registered his complaint by leaving his examination paper blank and writing a letter on the back. He pointed out that he had gone to work in the countryside and had had little time to do any studying. The examinations had come as a surprise and he had not been able to revise. He went on:

> To tell the truth, I have no respect for the bookworms who for many years have been taking it easy and have done nothing useful. I dislike them intensely. During the busy summer hoeing time, I just could not abandon my production task and hide myself in a small room to study. That would have been very selfish. If I had done that, I would have been guilty of being unworthy of the revolutionary cause which concerns both the poor and lower-middle peasants and myself . . ..

The whole tone of Zhang's letter implied that the reintroduction of examinations was undermining the ideals of the Cultural Revolution. Zhang's criticism was given nationwide publicity and led to a whole new campaign of attacks on the way the educational system was developing. People argued that the 'ghost of the old entrance examination system' had returned. Others pointed out that the children of cadres were once again getting entry to university education by their fathers pulling strings behind the scenes. Several students confessed that they had gained entry 'through the back door' in this way. As a result, the emphasis once more moved towards political standards and practical experience in the selection of students for university training.

University and college education still represents China's chief source of specialist manpower for modernisation. Until the Cultural Revolution, the quotas for the number of people studying a

54 *Teachers training at a Kwangtung college also do productive labour assembling oscilloscopes*

particular subject were centrally planned and most students had to accept the courses they were offered—though they could state their preference, and this might be taken into consideration. In the early 1960s approximately 40 per cent specialised in engineering, 22 per cent in education, and 13 per cent in medicine. The arts and social sciences received much less emphasis. Although no public announcements have been made, it seems likely that quotas for specialists will still be set with similar proportions as before. However, one new feature of the quota system is that universities and colleges must take a larger number of women, members of the national minorities and people from backward areas. Reports on enrolment in 1973 also indicated that as many as 80 per cent of new students are Party members.

In 1965, there were said to be 664 institutions of higher education in China. 43 were full universities offering a wide range of courses. 113 were teacher-training colleges, and the rest were specialist institutes. Over half of the specialist institutes taught industrial subjects such as metallurgy, mining, building construction, oil refining and so forth. The rest included medicine, agricultural studies, commercial subjects, foreign languages and the arts. Although the majority of these institutions still exist as the core of China's higher educational system, there has been a shift away from over-specialisation and towards more practical work. Many colleges have formed close links with industrial units. Students and staff spend a lot of their time working and experimenting at industrial sites, and new courses are developed which tie the universities to industrial processes. Colleges also do technical research on behalf of factories and all students do productive labour in college workshops. At Qinghua University in Peking, for example, the students produce lorries and computer controlled milling machines.

Outside of universities, there are a number of ways in which ordinary people can get further education, though slightly below university standard. The 'workers' universities' of the Great Leap Forward period have been revived. In addition, large factories have established training schemes to give technical training to their staff. Sometimes these are called colleges and form links with universities and institutes.

All universities are now headed by revolutionary committees. These are often subdivided into groups which take charge of different matters such as finance, educational reform, political work and general administration. Educational reform is the subject of constant discussion and every week meetings are held among the staff and students to consider how courses can be improved and how they can match political priorities more closely. In very large universities, there may also be revolutionary committees at faculty or departmental level. The division into faculties and academic departments with professors is maintained, though the professors have little administrative power. Until 1966, western academics who visited China reported that, apart from the social sciences, the quality of the work done was very high. In engineering, science and medicine, the best work equalled the best in other parts of the world. The few visitors since 1966 have also reported that standards are good, despite the drive to shorten courses from 4 to 3 years or less. However, the shift towards a greater integration of theory and practice and the increase in applied studies underlines that educational priorities are now more carefully defined in terms of immediate economic, political and social needs.

Within universities, students lead a very highly organised life. They all live on campus in large dormitory blocks with about half a dozen students to a room. Each term lasts five months with holidays in January and July. The students are divided into grades and classes, each with a full timetable of daily activity. Most classes have a class teacher who deals with tutorial work and personal problems. The following daily routine was recorded at the Kwangtung Teacher Training College in 1971, but it is almost exactly the same as that at the Sian Foreign Languages Institute where I taught in 1965.

0600 Reveille, followed by physical exercises.
0630 Radio broadcasts, news and comment.
0700 Breakfast.
0730 Daily study of Mao's works.
0830 Classes or productive labour.
1130 Free time.
1200 Lunch and siesta.
1430 Classes, private study, or labour.
1630 Extra-curricular activity, including sport, Communist Youth League work and so forth.
1730 Dinner.
1800 Free time.
1930 Newspaper reading and discussion.
2000 Private study.
2200 Lights out.

On Sundays, the students are free to do what they want and they usually make most of their own entertainment. In 1965 and 1966, I was regularly invited to join in or attend a performance, all of which were given with great enthusiasm and enjoyment. On the whole, the students showed no resentment over the way in which their life was planned. When I told them of the relative absence of pressures on students in Britain, they felt that the lack of structure and discipline could only lead to confusion and no sense of purpose. On the other hand, when my students became Red Guards, they sharply criticised the Party authorities for trying to make them into 'docile tools' who would follow the wrong political line.

Chinese students are extremely self-disciplined and hard working. Much of this derives from the extent to which political motivation is made part of everything they do from the time they first enter school. They are all trained to feel that their work serves a greater social purpose than their individual ambitions. When they encounter personal or vocational difficulties, the teachers and advisors always express their help and advice in political and ideological terms. In this way, the students learn to examine all their thoughts and actions in the light of the Party's principles and make a conscious effort to conform to them. At the same time, restrictions are placed on the amount of foreign or ideologically suspect materials available to students. At Qinghua University in 1971, the catalogue of western-language literature and philosophy was kept with the closed stacks. A check is also kept on a student's reading tendencies so as to guard against possible 'perversion' of his outlook. Nevertheless, in many university libraries, the staff organises criticism meetings and displays to draw attention to the defects of particular books, and it is believed that students must be allowed to read some questionable materials so as to learn to discriminate between good and bad. Otherwise, 'like hot-house flowers', they would be unable to survive outside their special environment.

The Teachers

Change has been a constant feature of teachers' lives since 1949. Sometimes the government or Party have introduced innovations suddenly and arbitrarily, and at other times the teachers have been able to influence decisions through discussion and consultation. The rapid expansion in education has led to a chronic shortage of staff despite the efforts of the training schools. As a result, the composition of the teaching body has altered considerably. The number of young trained teachers has greatly increased and so has the number of untrained and unqualified staff assimilated into the profession. In 1956, it was reported that there were 1,650,000 primary teachers and that another 1,170,000 would be needed by 1962, 500,000 more than the training schools could produce. The situation in secondary schools was even more desperate and many teachers trained for primary level were drafted upwards leaving the primaries to make up the deficit as best they could. The use of unqualified personnel to close the gap has not always been seen as a second-rate measure. In the part-time schools there has been no alternative. But during the Cultural Revolution, it was argued that it was an advantage to have people from all walks of life introduce their skills and experience into the class-room. Their help has been sought particularly for political and practical classes.

Changes in ideological climate have also profoundly affected teachers. Immediately after 1949, there was a period of adjustment during which they had to relinquish contacts with western countries and reorient towards the Soviet Union and communism. Thereafter the Party paid increasing attention to their individual political outlook. Teachers had to attend classes to study Marxism and criticise unorthodox attitudes. The prevailing policy was to use non-communist intellectuals while reforming them through study and periods of manual labour. With occasional changes in emphasis, this policy has remained in force until today. This has not created many problems for new recruits but for older teachers, especially those trained abroad many of whom are in senior positions, the transition has not been easy. Some like Ma Yin-chu, the President of Peking University until 1960, refused to change and lost their jobs. Others, like an American-trained former professor of sociology whom I met at Qinghua in 1971, decided that their particular approach was no longer acceptable and shifted to other work, in this case running the library. Most have realised that they now have to revise the ideological considerations underlying their work and conform to the new standards.

In normal times, political problems are dealt with by discussion and study groups within schools and colleges, but in mass campaigns there is often sharp criticism followed by painful public self-examination and confession. During the Cultural Revolution, large numbers of teachers went through this process. It left many reluctant to assume authority or make decisions which might lay them open to further criticism.

Teacher training is provided by full-time courses and a variety of correspondence and short courses. The latter are often given by groups of lecturers touring rural areas trying to improve the standards of the unqualified teachers. In addition, trained staff within schools supervise the new recruits. Pay and working conditions vary considerably. In universities, professors can earn as much as 400 *yuan* a month compared to the average lecturer's salary of 60. In the full-time schools, the highest salary is often around 150 *yuan*, the average 60, and the lowest 45. Teachers with college education are usually paid more than people with less training. Most teachers live in cheap accommodation within school and university compounds. They also get the benefit of comprehensive health and welfare schemes. In part-time schools, income is much lower. The teachers are treated as ordinary members of the unit where they work and receive the standard wage or workpoint distribution. Sometimes extra allowances are paid but there is pressure to keep the differences between teachers and other workers as low as possible. When this is combined with less training and the greater amount of practical work expected of them, the life of rural teachers is very different from their urban colleagues.

In the classroom, the teacher is both counsellor and educator. His methods are rather authoritarian and he relies to a great extent on careful planning and the provision of supplementary material. Before each course is taught, the teachers meet to discuss it and plan their approach. They list the most important items to be learnt and agree on the best methods of explanation and the best exercises. They also consider the political content and the way this should be underlined for the students. Finally they decide on the teaching aids they need. In this way there is a large degree of standardisation of teaching within an institution. Classroom presentation tends to be very serious with little improvisation or lightheartedness. Even the criticism of the Cultural Revolution has not undermined this. In 1973, a primary school student called Huang Shuai who lives in Peking wrote a letter to the newspaper attacking her teacher's strict discipline. She had kept a diary of advice for him and, as a result, had been criticised by him for 'being obstructive, for hurting his prestige, and for malicious attacks against him'. Here is her diary entry for 7 September:

> Today a certain pupil did not follow discipline in the class and was guilty of some petty and mean actions. You asked him to come forward and said: 'I really feel like hitting you on the head with my pointer'. Your words are not appropriate. The pointer is your tool for teaching students, not for hitting them on the head. I think you are making too many harsh criticisms of your students and giving them very little patient assistance. Can you solve the ideological problem just by striking the table and staring at us in anger? I hope you will patiently help the students when they have made mistakes, and pay more attention to what you are saying.

However, according to most reports, the formal style of teaching is not a hindrance to good relations between teachers and pupils. Instead, the teacher's position as moral guide—a status inherited from the past—does much to form a close bond with his pupils. Discipline is not a great problem and physical punishment is illegal.

The provision of good teachers is one of the fundamental problems of Chinese education. It is one which will increase as the process of technical modernisation makes greater demands for specialist training. However, through the use of untrained teachers and part-time schooling, the Chinese are experimenting with new ways of dealing with the problem.

Culture: Art and Ideology

For most of this century—starting well before the formation of the Communist Party—the arts in China have been experiencing a profound revolution. Foreign ideas and methods have challenged ancient traditions and forms, and China's artists and writers have worked to assimilate the new influences. Writers have abandoned the classical language as their medium of expression and developed styles closer to everyday speech. They have introduced the modern short story, the spoken play and new ways of writing poetry and novels. Painters have learnt the use of oils and other western techniques in order to give new forms of expression to their art. Musicians have adopted western instruments and musical forms alongside their own. At the same time, modern forms such as photography have been introduced. At the heart of this ferment has been a key debate over technique and content. While the technical side of western art has provided a wealth of new means of expression, there have always been reservations about the content. China's artists, communist and non-communist, have preferred to link their work to the political and social revolution going on around them.

The establishment of the People's Republic in 1949 provided a new framework for these developments characterised by greater concern with ideological problems and indigenous experiment than with foreign models. Strict limitations are now placed on the content and range of artistic thought and many pre-1949 artists and their works have been criticised and suppressed. Entertainment and artistic skills are the means used to convey a message

55 *A woodcut praises rural health workers*

and not ends in themselves. The guidelines are those laid down by Mao in his *Talks at the Yenan Forum on Literature and Art*, which he originally gave in 1942. Mao asks the artist to view his society and work in Marxist terms. He believes that the artist's duty is not merely to describe but to illustrate the inner meaning of reality from the Marxist point of view. The politically good should be praised, the weak encouraged, and the bad attacked. Mao also argues that in any society artistic and political standards are closely united and that the latter are most important. He denounces attitudes that separate art and politics, or conceive of artistic work as in any way independent and superior to productive labour. To get the right outlook, artists should study Marxism and work with ordinary people, learning to understand them and to use their language. Mao denies that all this may lead to dogmatic propaganda and destroy creativity on the grounds that Marxism is never dogmatic.

Apart from making artists conform to a particular ideology, these ideas have also created a great deal of tension in their lives. They face criticism should they oppose Mao and they have the uncertainties of working in a changing political situation where a new policy can render an old work liable to attack. Nevertheless, debate has not disappeared and various critics have attempted to challenge Mao's policies. This process has been marked by fluctuations between periods of relatively free debate and periods of tighter political control. In the relaxed discussions of 1954, the writer Hu Feng called for the complete removal of political restrictions on the arts. A few months later, the Party responded by alleging a political attack on the state and sentenced him to

56 *A play praises the use of acupuncture to cure deafness*

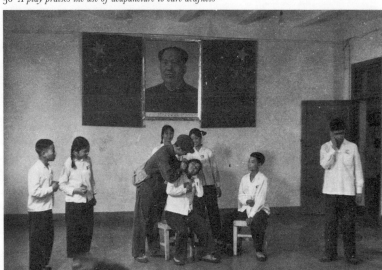

57 *A Peking cinema queue waits to see the model opera 'Taking Tiger Mountain'*

prison. Two years later, writers again called for more freedom for the artist to make his own interpretation of society, to use his own aesthetic standards and greater descriptive realism. This time they were accused of ideological mistakes and had to go through labour reform. The Cultural Revolution was another climax in these debates. It represented a shift back towards Mao's position after the relative relaxation of the early 1960s when artists were allowed slightly greater scope in their choice of themes.

Two other factors have complicated artistic debate since 1949. First, they have been used as a means of factional dispute between opposing literary groups. Until 1966, Zhou Yang, the former deputy director of the Party's Propaganda Department and deputy chairman of the Writers' Union, was able to manipulate artistic debate to further the interests of his own friends and associates. Hu Feng and others had put their criticisms forward in 1954 partly in the hope of replacing Zhou's group with their own.

Secondly, artistic effort is very often used as a means of political criticism. An apparently innocuous play can be the vehicle for a sharp attack on a particular policy or person. The historical essays, dramas and anecdotes written by Wu Han, Deng Tuo and others between 1960 and 1962 were not simply works of art. They were disguised criticisms of the policies pursued by Mao Ze-dong. For example, Wu Han's play, *The Dismissal of Hai Rui*, used the story of a Ming Dynasty official's opposition to the emperor's rural policies as an analogy to attack Mao's drive to establish people's communes. Hai Rui was described as a loyal official who was generous to the ordinary peasants. He attempted to stop the usurpation of land by the gentry. However, the emperor refused to listen and dismissed him. In his introduction, Wu Han said that this story had 'lessons for today'. The parallel between the historical situation and the introduction of the communes by the Party was obvious and this was made even more explicit by the fact that Peng De-huai, a Party leader, had attempted to criticise Mao for the difficulties faced by the peasants and was forced to resign. In this way, the political implications of the story far outweighed its artistic value, though no-one outside China unravelled what was going on until it was explained by the Red Guards in 1966.

The Model Operas

Chinese opera is not the specialist interest that opera is in the west. It is enthusiastically supported by people at all levels of society and all performances are always sold out. Each area of China has its own local form. After the Cultural Revolution began, all pre-1949 operas were criticised and no longer performed, and doubts were raised about many others that had been produced during the previous 20 years. Apart from a large number of songs and dances in modern and traditional styles devoted to praising Mao, communism and the Red Guards, little else was produced. The only major developments were a few modern revolutionary operas and ballets. The operas were derived from traditional Peking style with western musical innovations and modernised presentation. They combined singing, dancing, acrobatics and drama. The ballets owed much to the classical Russian style. They were not all entirely new, having been developed since 1964 under Jiang Qing, Mao's wife, but as revised after 1966 they came to represent model works of art setting standards for others to copy.

A typical plot is that of the opera, *The Red Lantern*, summarised as follows in the Chinese magazine *China Reconstructs*:

The Red Lantern takes place in an enemy-held city during the War of Resistance against Japanese aggression.

Li Yu-he, a railway switchman, is a member of the Chinese Communist Party and a seasoned underground worker. He and his mother and daughter are actually from three different worker families, brought together during the 7 February 1923 railway strike.

From a higher Party organisation Li Yu-he receives a secret code which he must deliver to the guerrillas in the Cypress Mountains. Before he can fulfil his mission, he is betrayed to the chief of the Japanese gendarmes, Hatoyama, who invites him to a 'feast', tries persuasion and threat and then arrests and tortures him to make him give up his code. But the Communist meets the enemy with unflinching courage. Both at the feast and on the execution ground, he defeats Hatoyama with righteous rage. At his wits' end, Hatoyama executes Li Yu-he and his mother, Granny Li.

Li's daughter, Tie-mei, takes over the mission from her martyred father. Led by the Party and helped by her neighbours, she succeeds in delivering the secret code to the guerrillas.

This opera shares certain general characteristics with the other models. It is the work of a group of people rather than an individual and it has been revised several times to make adjustments in the political emphasis. It is set in recent times and dwells on the struggle between good and bad, both expressed in sharply black-and-white terms. The hero is of good class origin and displays all the virtues expected of a communist, with no real weaknesses. 'Middle' characters—those with inner conflicts neither entirely good nor entirely bad—are not included, and there is no interest in personal romance or salvation. The ending is positive.

Although this may seem very stereotyped, it must be seen in its cultural context. The traditional Peking and local operas have always dwelt extensively on moral issues in a very simplistic way. The audience's main interest lay as much in the skill and virtuosity of the performance as in the content. The same reactions can be observed today. Particular scenes are anticipated with as much excitement as the entire plot. The merits of various actors in leading roles are keenly debated and one actor's presentation is often taken as the standard performance. Key excerpts are put on at concerts and by amateur groups.

Until 1971, these models displaced all local operas and were virtually the only theatrical works performed. Since then all new productions have followed their general features, though it was indicative of the continuing use of art for political ends that a play from Shansi Province was denounced in 1974 for attempting to defend the rural policies of the long disgraced Liu Shao-qi.

The Literary Scene

As with the operas, little new work was published for a long time after 1966. Many writers were reluctant to take up their pens again for fear that they might suffer further criticism. However, encouragement in the press led to a steady flow of new works after 1971. New writings concentrate almost exclusively on workers, peasants and soldiers. Writers are encouraged to go out and work among ordinary people and to reflect their lives when they write. In 1973, a leading novelist, Hao Ran, described his approach to writing:

> The fundamental difference between bourgeois writers and us centres on the question of whether literature should be for the amusement of the comfortably off, and deal with the so-called 'inner world' and sentiments of the bourgeoisie, or whether it should truly present the workers, the peasants and other working people who are the motive force in the making of world history. Can the 'eternal themes' of the bourgeoisie concerning 'love' and 'death' match those of the great struggles of the working masses? A western journalist once asked me, 'why don't you play up the theme of love between men and women?' I replied: there is love in life indeed. But in a class society, love is inevitably stamped with the brand of a class. What to love and how to express one's love? In this respect a poor peasant and a landlord have nothing in common. Love is only presented when it is relevant and necessary to the theme and characterisation.

Hao Ran is a poor peasant by origin and only had three years of schooling. He began to write in 1957. Before publishing he circulates his drafts among workers and peasants for criticism, on the basis of which he makes his revisions. He also comments on other's manuscripts and gives coaching to amateur writers.

One of the most prominent literary forms today is reportage, in which an author imaginatively describes an actual event in the form of a short story. The bare facts are embroidered and idealised. This form is used for most subject matter, from the war in Vietnam to the struggle for development in the model commune, Dazhai. Its style is barely distinguishable from that of the short story which, though entirely imaginative also concentrates on typical modern events and problems. In fact, there is a direct relationship between literary output and current social problems and policies, even though the story is always ideal and conclusions are never unhappy or politically unsatisfactory as they might be in real life. A drive to move urban youth to the countryside will be accompanied by stories and poems dealing with the effect on family life and the problems of settling down in a new environment. The continuing fight for female emancipation is illustrated by stories of how women have to overcome the obstacles raised by their menfolk. Conflicts of interest between individual peasants and the collective are echoed in stories that tell how they were resolved. In this way, literature does give insight into the problems which social change is generating and the way in which they are overcome.

The increase in new publications after 1971 was accompanied by greater freedom for traditional literature and classical studies. Some of the old novels were republished and some of the dynastic histories. Visitors to China reported that these were being eagerly bought, reflecting a continuing interest in the literary heritage of the past. In addition, magazines devoted to archeology and classical culture were republished. Limitations are still placed on the extent of these interests and all evaluation must be done on the basis of Marxist ideas but, despite the criticisms of the Red Guards, the Chinese are clearly proud of their great cultural traditions.

The Visual Arts

Once again, the political situation dictates the subject matter. Revolutionary themes predominate, and only during periods of greater relaxation is there more opportunity to handle others. The emphasis is on forms that have a mass appeal and reflect everyday life and the new morality. Highly intellectual, abstract art is not practised and, as far as can be seen, does not interest

58 *Basketball in a village—a watercolour done by a peasant artist*

Chinese artists who work within their own traditional symbolic forms and old impressionistic styles. Combined with new techniques imported from abroad, this gives the Chinese painter great scope for different forms of presentation. Thus, pictures in many different styles illustrate the significance of a new policy or major event. A painter using old Chinese materials is often able to make his point in a muted way—as when the modernisation of the countryside is shown by a small factory in the corner of an old-fashioned landscape. One using the 'socialist realist' style of poster painting will boldly overstate his message, distorting proportions and detail.

Heroic themes are sometimes treated in oils and sometimes in derived traditional forms. Symbolism is widely used with such devices as a rising red sun to indicate Mao and a pine tree to mean longevity. Stress on folk arts has led to an upsurge in such things as woodcuts and paper-cuts. These are used for traditional effects as well as to convey contemporary images. On the whole, a careful look at Chinese pictorial art, from major works to trivial illustrations, can tell a lot about current preoccupations in the country. An interesting exercise for the reader would be to compare the pictures in a copy of *Chinese Literature* of 1967 with those of 1973. The differences will provide him with some insights into the role of pictorial art in China and the nature of Chinese society.

The Artist

For political reasons the amateur artist in China receives a great deal of encouragement. The fact that the mass media and other forms of commercial entertainment are not so widely available as in other countries gives him an added status. Almost everyone seems able and prepared to contribute something by singing, dancing, or playing an instrument. Large numbers try their hand at writing and painting. If they wish they can submit their efforts to local or national publications for printing and in that event they receive a fee. Occasionally good amateurs are given widespread publicity and their works become nationally famous.

Professionals, on the other hand, often go through a long period of training to perfect their skills. Promising youngsters are sent to special schools which concentrate on their talents. They are then able to attend academies and conservatories at university level where they do intensive courses. After graduating, many are given jobs within their fields. Actors and musicians join theatres and orchestras. Others are given cultural or educational posts, such as work in publishing houses or in universities. They not only practise their art but also devote some of their time to its administration or to teaching it. A writer, for example, might

59 *A pottery near Canton produces figures of the characters from the opera 'The Red Lantern'*

work in the publishing department of the Writers' Union editing and reading manuscripts, as well as producing his own works. All writers of any standing belong to this Union, to which they submit their works for critical comment and publication. It is in this process that political problems are ironed out and works revised if necessary. Without approval by this or similar bodies, it would be impossible for a writer or other artist to publish or produce, since there are no underground magazines circulating in the country. Apart from their normal wages, writers also receive a fee for published work but this is not large and there are no royalties or copyright restrictions.

Undoubtedly many artists have felt oppressed by the current political role of art. They have also argued that the level of creative work is low. However, many others are more concerned with building up new forms of mass expression and with the problem of social development. They put these issues before purely aesthetic considerations.

6
Some Special Citizens

In this book, I have tried to draw the broad outlines of life in China. Inevitably, I have been forced to omit much that gives colour and character to the daily activities of the Chinese people. The bicycle-taxi drivers' regular game of chess while waiting for customers, the goldfish collectors' delight in the exotic species that have long had a special place among China's traditional hobbies, the huge, chirping crickets in bamboo cages which the peasants bring into town to sell during the hot summer months, the old men taking their pet birds for walks and hanging the cages on park trees while they chat with their friends—the catalogue of such things is endless. They are part of the trivia of life, yet they add to its texture and mean much to the people involved. Moreover, there are many professions and social groups which do not fit easily into broad generalisations about Chinese society. Many of these groups, though small in themselves, have important roles to play in the social structure. Others stand outside the mainstream of life and are remarkable for that very reason. Previous chapters have concentrated on the more typical features of Chinese society. In this chapter I shall fill in some of the gaps by looking at a few of China's more significant social minorities.

'A Farewell to the God of Plague'
Serving the health needs of more than 800 million people requires a considerable investment both in men and materials. Doctors, midwives, chemists, nurses and medical orderlies have to be trained, hospitals and clinics built and equipped, and medicines produced. In 1949, China had an estimated 180,000 medical and health workers trained in western medicine, of whom around

40,000 were doctors. This was equivalent to roughly one doctor for every 14,000 people. There were also some 84,000 hospital beds, or one for every 6,500 people. However, even this paltry provision was not equally shared by all. Most personnel and services were concentrated in the cities. In rural areas western medicine was almost unknown. The peasants could only rely on traditional Chinese medicine which, although rich in its use of herbs and acupuncture, lacked the basic knowledge of the body and of disease which has made western medicine so successful. More-over, traditional doctors were not systematically trained nor equally skilled. Many were little more than quacks capitalising on the superstitions of the uneducated peasants. Hand in hand with this lack of trained health workers went low standards of sanitation and hygiene. Infectious diseases such as smallpox, cholera and typhoid were widespread, as well as parasitic ill-nesses like malaria, schistosomiasis, and intestinal worms. In this situation, simple health education combined with improved sanitation could by themselves remove much of the threat to the people's health. However, the work could not be done without a government with the power and will to undertake it. As a result, the annual death rate for the whole population was more than 30 per 1,000, and some 275 out of every 1,000 children born did not survive their first few years.

After 1949, the new government adopted three main policies to deal with its medical problems. It increased the number of people being trained as doctors and health workers. It launched widespread campaigns for the enforcement of preventative measures and for general health education. And it encouraged the integration of western medicine and scientifically analysed traditional medicine. The guiding principles behind these policies stressed putting prevention before cure, serving the rural areas, and integrating public health work with mass movements. Resources were thus directed towards the areas with the greatest needs, while the mobilisation of the whole population in campaigns for cleanliness and the eradication of pests eliminated some of the sources of disease and led to a greater general understanding of medical principles.

During the first ten years of the People's Republic, there was a rapid growth in the number of trained medical workers. By 1959, the total was around 480,000, of whom 80,000 were fully qualified in western medicine. This was roughly one doctor for every 8,700 people. At the same time the number of hospital beds had risen to 440,000, or 1 for every 1,500 people. No reliable information on the number of medical workers has been issued for the years since 1959. The most recent general statement came in May 1973, when China's spokesman at the World Health Assembly in Geneva stated that 'the total number of hospital beds in China has increased by 19 times as compared with that before liberation' and 'the total number of college-graduated medical and health workers trained since the founding of the People's Republic of China is 27 times that trained in the 20 years before liberation'. As the basis for these figures was not given, it is difficult to draw any conclusions from them beyond the general implication that medical services have continued to expand at a rapid rate.

Although the rate of growth of medical services has steadily accelerated since 1949, there has been a marked change in the relative emphasis given to different kinds of medical training. Until the late 1960s, preference was given to a long and thorough education in western medicine. Doctors were trained in much the same way as they are trained in western countries. The large teaching hospitals, many originally founded by missionaries, remained the key centres of medical skills. Although health campaigns did much to improve the situation in the countryside, there was still a tendency to neglect the expansion of basic medicine in the rural areas in favour of concentration on modern techniques in the cities. During the Cultural Revolution, the emphasis shifted to the training of medical orderlies and less highly qualified doctors capable of using both western and Chinese medicine to treat simple illnesses. Their function is to spread basic medical services throughout the countryside, and to deal with the prevention and cure of common ailments. They also give lessons in birth control as part of the national drive to reduce the rate of population growth. Most of these medical workers are expected to spend part of their time at productive work in factories and communes. They are called 'barefoot doctors' because, like ordinary peasants, they can be found working barefoot in the paddy fields. 'Barefoot doctor' courses are open to anyone who has aptitude and comes from an area of need. They do not have to sit special entrance examinations. Their training lasts up to two years and includes such things as basic anatomy, physiology,

60 *A Mongolian 'barefoot doctor' does her rounds on the steppeland, visiting the yurts which are moved to follow the herds of cows and horses*

pathology, and knowledge of Chinese traditional medicine and medicinal herbs, common diseases and their causes, and basic surgery. When they meet cases beyond their abilities, they are expected to refer to more expert advice. The following report shows how doctors from a county hospital who went on a duty tour of rural areas helped to train some 'barefoot doctors' in 1965.

The urban doctors stayed in the mountain villages for two months, and even at the time of their departure people kept coming for some kind of treatment or operation. They realised that it was imperative to train doctors to work in the villages. So when they returned to the town they took along with them two young persons from the commune clinic.

Two experienced doctors were detailed to coach them. They had their charges with them, whether inspecting the wards, diagnosing, operating or changing dressings, patiently initiating them into the finer points of their calling. Barely 20, these youths studied and read books diligently. After one year they could handle common surgical cases, do appendectomies and repair hernias.

Dr Wang said: 'Since then we have been employing this method to train one or two surgeons for each commune clinic. The same method has also been used to train personnel for other branches of medicine. We have also set up a health school to train health workers for the communes and brigades. In recent years, the practice has been to train about 100 trainees at a time; one half study in class while the other half get practical experience in the wards. Generally speaking the course is for two years. We also go down to the countryside to help them improve their work after they get back.'

Whatever the quality of the 'barefoot doctors', and clearly they are not trained to deal with rare or complex illnesses, their efforts are doing much to improve the standards of public health. In this work, they are helped by the large mass campaigns to spread preventative measures. These campaigns are run like any other mass movement. General propaganda is issued in the media and reflected in the arts and literature. Small group meetings are held where activists strive to work up popular enthusiasm. Eventually people are mobilised to carry out the intended work. As a result of these campaigns, which have been organised regularly since 1949—most often in the spring before the warm weather arrives, the incidence of diseases like schistosomiasis has greatly declined. The following report of June 1959, describes the work of such a campaign in Anhwei Province.

In the first ten days of June, a short-term shock campaign centred round the extermination of mosquitoes and flies was launched in Anhwei in combination with the accumulation of manure. In town and country, garbage was cleared, weeds were eliminated, ditches were dredged, and ponds were filled up. Poisonous wild plants were collected to kill flies and mosquitoes; maggots in latrines and cesspools were destroyed. In the surburban areas of Jieshou, 17,800 hundredweight of garbage was cleared and 196 hollow areas were filled up in two days. In Maanshan municipality, 1,400,000 hundredweight of weeds were eliminated and 11,000 hundredweight of manure was accumulated for the communes in the course of clearing night-soil and garbage and dredging ditches. According to incomplete statistics, 17,000 hundredweight of poisonous wild plants were collected and maggots in 11,000 latrines and cesspools were destroyed in some areas of Shexian. In Wuhu municipality, over 20,000 piles of wild plants were set on fire to fumigate 120,000 rooms.

To prevent gastro-intestinal diseases during the summer, energetic measures have been taken in Anhwei to insure clean food and drinks. Urban food and drink trades instituted hygiene systems and strict check-ups. Employees of the food and drink trades in Wuhu municipality have formed the habit of wearing masks and frequently washing hands. 32,000 rural mess halls in the Wuhu administrative district have generally provided facilities to keep flies and dust away from food. Over 20,000 cooks in Suixi County have been given instruction in general hygiene.

At the other end of the scale, China's surgeons have experimented with and introduced sophisticated new techniques. Paralleling the national political emphasis on the role of working people, they have concentrated on the treatment of industrial and other work injuries. They have been particularly successful with operations to rejoin severed limbs or fingers and with the handling of exceptionally severe burns. In a case widely reported in 1973, for example, surgeons joined a woman's right foot to her left leg after a railway accident in which her right leg and left foot were crushed. During these treatments, the doctors have not only developed techniques along western lines but they have also used traditional herbal and acupuncture treatment. It is in this extension of the use of traditional medicine that the most startling developments have taken place in Chinese medicine.

China's use of medicinal herbs is based on a long, empirical

61 *A Chinese chemist weighs out herbal medicines*

tradition. Over many centuries, traditional doctors have effectively developed herbal remedies for many illnesses without knowing the scientific basis for their success. Contemporary research is showing that in fact a lot of these herbs contain chemicals with important medicinal uses. Formerly most of the plants involved were wild and many grew in remote areas. Their collection was often haphazard and risky. Now they are being cultivated by communes. After the plants, nuts, leaves, seeds or flowers have been harvested, they are preserved either by drying or crushing. The herbal chemist's shop is crammed with bottles and drawers full of strange, shrivelled plants and exotic smells. Sometimes the chemists themselves prepare prescriptions, making up small balls of chewy medicine with strong and often repulsive flavours. More commonly, the traditional doctor makes out a list of ingredients which are carefully weighed out by the chemist and bought by the patient. The patient then takes them home, boils them up, and drinks the end product. The following recipe is recommended as a cure for coughs with congestion, panting and fluctuations in temperature.

	drachms
Xuanfu flower petals (inula japonica Thunb.)	4
Dried Jingjie flower (Schizonepeta tenuifolia Briq.)	2
Angelica root (Peucedanum praeruptorum Dunn)	2
Preparation from the stalks of Banxia (Pinellia ternata Breit.)	3
Dried Xixin (Asarum heterotropoides F.Schum.)	3

Boil and drink.

Acupuncture is based on the use of fine needles up to ten inches long which are inserted at special points on the body. According to traditional theory, these points are linked by meridians along which flow blood and 'vital energy'. Each point is said to be related to a specific organ or illness. Altogether several hundred points are in use. After the doctor has made his diagnosis, he inserts needles in several points for a period of time. Sometimes they are heated or agitated at intervals. During this process the patient feels no pain. The treatment for rheumatism, for example, involves points on the wrists, feet and stomach. In the past, acupuncture was mainly used to treat chronic illnesses such as circulatory and respiratory problems, arthritis, and headaches, though claims were made for its effectiveness against malaria,

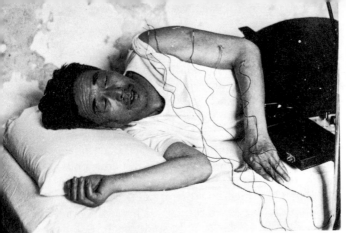

62 *Acupuncture with electric current is used to treat rheumatism*

dysentery and a variety of other ailments. So far, the exact limits within which acupuncture is truly effective have not been measured by modern methods.

As yet there has been no scientific explanation for the effects of acupuncture. The old 'meridian' theory is not supported by any discovery of a system like the nervous system through which the 'vital energy' could flow. However, early in 1974 Chinese doctors reported that they had measured changes in chemical activity in the brain during the use of acupuncture and, though their research is in its early stages, it seems possible that these changes may be an essential part of the reason why acupuncture works.

Since the early 1960s, much of the research into acupuncture has concentrated on its regulatory effects on the system. It has been found to slow the heartbeat, provide sedation and relieve pain. Many of these effects can be increased by the passing of small electric currents through the needles. The most important development came in the late 1960s when acupunctural techniques were discovered that provide an alternative form of anaesthetisation. One or two needles inserted in a few selected points can remove all feeling of pain in related parts of the body for up to nine hours. Using this simple technique, Chinese surgeons have been able to carry out long and complicated operations such as open-heart surgery, pneumonectomy, removal of stomach ulcers and so forth. During the operations, patients are fully conscious and can cooperate with the surgeon if necessary. It is claimed that convalescence is quicker and easier with this method, and that all the bad effects of general anaesthesia on the body can be avoided.

At the very least it is cheap, easy to use, and makes surgical work in remote, ill-equipped country clinics much more feasible. Acupuncture anaesthesia has therefore become a technique widely used by doctors of many different levels of training. Its use is being intensively studied and extended.

Medical services are not free but charges are kept very low. The removal of an appendix can cost as little as 8 *yuan* (less than £2) and child delivery around 2 *yuan*. A major operation such as brain surgery costs 30 *yuan*. Medicines, x-rays and other services are also charged for. A chest x-ray works out at about 0.30 *yuan* and an ampoule of 200,000 units of penicillin about 0.14 *yuan*. In November 1972, one Chinese journal estimated that the medical expenses of a child hospitalised with pneumonia for eight days would be 16 *yuan*. In addition, hospital patients have to pay for their food. However, few Chinese have to pay all their medical expenses themselves. Full-time productive workers receive complete medical insurance as part of their work and their families get 50 per cent cover. Peasants usually belong to a cheap insurance scheme run by their commune which costs one to two *yuan* per year. Only the dependents of non-productive workers, such as government office workers, are not directly covered by some form of insurance. During the early 1970s, city districts began experimenting with neighbourhood insurance schemes to cover this group. Most Chinese are well pleased with the vast improvement in the quality and provision of health services that has taken place since 1949.

Scientific Workers

The Chinese approach to scientific research firmly rejects the idea of the pure researcher working on the frontiers of theoretical knowledge within the confines of his laboratory. Instead, the overwhelming emphasis is placed on applied science that can bring immediate results in production. The scientist is not thought of as a member of an elite intellectual class dedicated to some higher ideal, but as a man who goes out into factories and farms where he solves practical problems or develops new ideas in cooperation with the ordinary working man.

There are two main reasons for this attitude. On the one hand the Chinese believe that 'science is a product of practice', that 'natural science arises from man's knowledge of natural laws and is the product of experience in production struggle and scientific experimentation. It is definitely not the result of the hypotheses of men divorced from practice.' On the other hand, the immediate economic needs of the country do not permit large investment in basic research. China cannot afford to compete with richer countries in areas of limited practical application. Even if it could, it has not yet developed the social, institutional and industrial structures that could quickly translate basic research into productive technological processes. As a result, China's scientists are asked to concentrate their efforts on developing a technology to suit the Chinese environment and adapting scientific knowledge that comes from abroad to conform to China's needs.

Not all of China's scientists have been happy with this role. Many were trained abroad and returned to China in the years after 1949. They were used to the idea of independent research, and they placed a premium on the extension of basic, theoretical knowledge. The Communist Party has constantly argued against this attitude, instituted campaigns for reeducation, and made reforms to ensure that scientists spend much of their time working on practical production problems. In 1971, two American biolgists went to China and talked with Chinese scientists including one known to them from before 1949, who had studied in America. Loo Shih-wei (their spelling) was then 64 and they reported on what he told them of his attitude to his work.

He is still a plant physiologist at the Institute of the Academia Sinica in Shanghai. He used to work in the laboratory on the effects of plant hormones on growth and on the development of agriculturally important plants. Since the Cultural Revolution he has been working on similar problems, but now he works in collaboration with members of a production brigade at Malu People's Commune just outside Shanghai. Like other western trained plant physiologists, he knew that the hormone gibberellin applied to seedlings increases the rate of plant growth but frequently not the final yield. However, at the suggestion of some of the peasants at the commune he tried applying it to barley at the flowering stage instead and found a 20 per cent increase in the yield of grain. Since purified gibberellin is expensive, he and the commune members together worked out a new technique, using a cheap, crude gibberellin preparation that they could make themselves. Loo says that he has felt much more socially useful since his 'reorientation' and is enjoying his work more. He cites his own case as evidence that scientists can frequently receive good suggestions from relatively untrained workers whose common sense has been sharpened by practical experience. He maintains that this did not happen before the Cultural Revolution because of the separation of intellectuals from average people. The Americans found that most of the research in the institutes they visited was directed towards improving production and integrating scientific workers with ordinary workers.

The overall planning of scientific research is in the hands of the State Council. This defines the main areas of work and directs where the greatest efforts should be made. The actual research is carried out through subordinate bodies of which the most important is the Chinese Academy of Sciences, which was set up in 1949. This has five departments: 1) physics, mathematics, and chemistry; 2) technical sciences; 3) philosophy and social sciences; 4) geology and geography; and 5) biological sciences. Each of these departments runs a number of regional branches and research institutes, staffed with the most able scientific manpower. In 1958, there were reported to be 170 institutes with a total staff of 28,300, of whom some 5,900 were actively engaged in research. Most attention is paid to applied science within the natural sciences. The social sciences are relatively neglected. In addition, some basic work is done and a notable achievement was the total synthesis of biologically active insulin at the Biochemical Institute in Shanghai in 1965. Outside of the Academy, research work is also undertaken by universities and other educational institutions, and by research bodies attached to central ministries or their enterprises. In the latter case, the work done is defined by the area of interest of the ministry concerned. The full total of research personnel in 1958 was 32,500 working in some 848 research establishments. Numbers have undoubtedly increased rapidly since then but no more recent figures have been given.

Equally as important as the top levels of research in China, there is a considerable effort to spread general scientific knowledge among the population. Organisations such as the China Association for Dissemination of Scientific and Technical Knowledge, the

Chinese Federation of Scientific Societies, and the Scientific and Technical Association of China have set up branches, committees and teams which actively work to raise the level of scientific awareness among the population at large. Although the standards aimed at are not high, they do contribute to the growth of scientific and technical skills. Their practical effect is realised in the national drive to introduce 'innovations'. Everyone is encouraged to put forward his ideas for the technical improvement of his work. If they are found to be useful, these ideas are put into practice. 'Innovations' cover all fields of work from improved ways of stacking goods in a warehouse to better machine design or a new way of feeding pigs. Simple improvements like these are regularly reported in the Chinese press and reflect the advance of technical skills among the community at large. In a sense, these innovators are also members of the scientific community.

Opinions on the quality and potential of scientific research in China vary considerably. Mikhail Klochko, a Soviet scientist who worked in China in the late 1950s, thought that the quality of China's researchers was as good as that of people in other countries. In fact he felt that China's scientists could soon outstrip those of the Soviet Union if they were allowed to get on with their work. However, he believed that the preference for applied science, the Communist Party's distrust of intellectuals, the copying of the Soviet system for planning scientific work, and the lack of contact with scientists in foreign countries were all stumbling blocks holding the Chinese back. By contrast, the American scientists quoted above did not feel that the Chinese were really cut off from foreign scientific work. Wherever they went, they found research institutes well stocked with the latest scientific literature from western countries. The people they talked to were also familiar with current work abroad connected with their subjects. The Americans felt that the emphasis on applied science was sound in view of the immediate problems facing the country. They were aware that political pressures had disrupted scientific work during the Cultural Revolution and that there had been a short-term loss in scientific productivity. But the laboratories they visited were working 'at a reasonable level' and they were interested in the long-term impact of the new relationship between scientists and workers. As regards the actual laboratories,

. . . most of the equipment was made in China, and appeared

to be of high quality. The laboratories themselves, scrupulously clean and neat, were furnished modestly, and very much resembled photographs of biology and chemistry laboratories in the United States in the 1920s and 1930s. This was true even in the laboratory where insulin was synthesised.

On the whole most scientists visiting China have been impressed by what they have seen. China's success with insulin and the rapid development of its nuclear weapons show that the Chinese can achieve high standards of research when the effort is needed. However until the country is much richer, most resources will be directed towards research which helps production, and China's scientists will have to build their careers around such work.

Religion

Religious beliefs have not presented any major ideological challenge to the Chinese Communist Party. Generally speaking, the Chinese have always been more concerned with the problems of social morality than with questions of religious faith, and there was no organised religion to oppose the new regime in 1949. Religion only had important social significance in the non-Chinese, national minority areas, where it reinforced racial and other cultural distinctions. The Party was therefore happy to include the right of freedom of religious faith in its state constitution. It believed that the growth of the new social order combined with widespread education in communist thought would quickly lead to the decline of the small religious communities. In many ways it has been proved true. However, toleration of religious belief has also been accompanied by active anti-religious propaganda. People who are religious are discriminated against and get little chance for social advancement. During periods of political mobilisation such as during the Cultural Revolution, they have been sharply criticised and prevented from worshipping. The official attitude was summed up in one journal in 1965 as,

. . . religion will not disappear of its own accord, it will rely on the force of custom to prolong its feeble existence and even plot to make a comeback. When a dying cobra bites a man, it can still wound or kill him. Therefore no matter how little of religion's vestigal poison remains, it is necessary to carry on a rigorous struggle against it on all fronts and to pull up and destroy all of its poisonous roots.

Today most religions are only supported by a declining number of old people and the young are rarely involved.

After 1949, the Communist Party reorganised the four main faiths, Christianity, Taoism, Buddhism, and Islam, into National Associations. These stressed their patriotic support for the new government, and attempted to draw parallels between the Communist Party's programme and their own religious ideals. They also played a role in foreign affairs by providing a means of contact with religious groups in other countries. This was particularly true of the Islamic and Buddhist Associations which participated in activities in the Middle East and Asia respectively. During the 1950s young Chinese moslems went to Mecca and Buddhist relics were sent abroad. However, these religious exchanges ceased during the 1960s when China's relations with the countries concerned became very strained.

Christianity is the weakest of all the religions in China. In 1949, there were only 800,000 Protestants and around 3 million Catholics, totaling less than 1 per cent of the population. The Church's close association with foreign invasion and control has also made it the most vulnerable to criticism. During the early years of the Republic, the Communists acted swiftly to expel all foreign clergy and missionaries. In the case of the Catholic Church, these accounted for more than 40 per cent of the priesthood. The foreign missionaries were also accused of spying, sabotage, and even atrocities against the Chinese people. Some were tried and jailed. The Party then set up two Patriotic Associations, one for the Protestants and one for the Catholics. The Protestants were more willing to accept this change than the Catholics who had to break with the Vatican and appoint their own priests. Their Association did not meet formally until 1956. The new Associations provided the framework for administering and controlling the Christian community. They were headed by emminent Christians but also had appointees of the Party. They enshrined the principles of self-government (i.e. the appointment of their own clergy), self-support (i.e. they had to rely on their own resources), and self-propagation (i.e. they could not try to convert others).

In 1965, I visited a Protestant church in Sian. It was run by a committee with a chairman, a manager, and a pastor. They told me there were 1,400 Protestants in the city (population $1\frac{1}{2}$

million) with 5 pastors and 10 preachers. There were also 3 Catholic priests. The church I visited had been a Baptist church before 1949 but afterwards all the Protestant churches had been combined. Church income came from the collections made at services and from the rent charged for the houses it owned. The rent was government controlled but, as a special favour, it was free of tax. The form of service, the hymns, and music were still exactly the same as those used in Britain. I was told that weddings and baptisms were very rare, but that there were occasional funerals. During the Cultural Revolution, this church was closed down by the Red Guards. Its rooftop crosses were taken away and a display of anti-Christian propaganda put up outside it. When I revisited the city in 1971, the building had been converted into offices. My impression was that Christianity is fast dying out in China. It seems unlikely that the faith will long outlive the generations converted by foreigners before 1949.

The Taoist religion, which is indigenous to China, had already lost much of its intellectual strength by 1949. It had become the preserve of individualists and recluses. As a popular religion it was full of superstition and Buddhist influences. It encompassed a wide variety of gods and local spirits. Nevertheless, it has been tolerated in the same way as the other religions. Until 1966, most large cities had Taoist temples with small groups of monks, and in the countryside the religion was still able to draw on a lingering reservoir of peasant superstition and support. At the holy mountain, Huashan, I found all the temples still functioning and groups of peasants climbing up the steep paths to visit them and enjoy the scenery. In general only the elderly were making offerings and burning incense, but I also saw some youths bowing before the statues of the gods. Most of the monks wore traditional clothes and only one had adopted modern dress. He told me that Mao had summed up and developed the essence of the Taoist beliefs, an opinion which indicates the efforts to bring Taoism to terms with the new communist ideology. Taoist temples were closed during the Cultural Revolution, and in some cases their contents were destroyed. However, many relics of important historical or cultural value were collected and stored in museums.

Buddhism has retained much more vigour than Taoism, one of the reasons being that in minority areas like Tibet and Inner Mongolia, Lama Buddhism is still popular and strongly supported.

63 *A former Taoist temple at Hangchow was converted into a class education exhibition during the Cultural Revolution*

Like Taoism, its greatest strength is in the countryside. When I visited them in 1965, the monks in the Xing Jiao Temple some 20 kilometres from Sian and in the Qi Xia Temple a similar distance from Nanking were leading a normal religious life and were active in the local community. But even within cities, Buddhism still functioned. Ordinary citizens could go and make offerings for the dead and hear the sutras chanted. The greater strength of Buddhism than Taoism also led to the founding of a Chinese Buddhist Institute in 1956, and leading Buddhists gained greater prominence in bodies like the National People's Congress. Nevertheless, the Buddhist faith has met with the same criticisms as the other religions. Few young people are converted to it. In 1966, Neale Hunter, an Australian teaching in China, visited the White Horse Temple near Loyang.

I was with a group of foreigners and we were talking, through interpreters, to a monk. One of the questions put to him was:

'And what do you monks do with your time?'

'We work in the field,' he replied. 'And we meditate.'

'Meditate?' asked one of the foreigners. 'What do you meditate on?'

The monk did not hesitate:

'I, myself,' he said, 'am working on the problem of *who* eats when *I* eat, *who* talks when *I* talk.'

This answer, which would be perfectly comprehensible to Buddhists anywhere in the world, was the source of much embarrassed and apologetic amusement among the interpreters—Shanghai students brought up almost entirely under the new regime. At first, they said the monk's words were unintelligible. When some of the foreigners insisted on a translation, they gave one but made it clear that such ideas were completely strange to them.

Most young people in China probably feel that they do not need religion any more. It is so out of touch with the spirit of their new society that it must seem like a dead language, which there is no reason to learn.

During the Cultural Revolution, Buddhism met the same fate as other religions. Temples were closed, monks were sent off to the countryside, and all devotions stopped. *Modern Buddhism*, the journal of the Chinese Buddhist Association, ceased publication. Many Buddhists were publically criticised and some of them were forced to get married and to eat meat.

Islam with some 10 million adherents mainly belonging to the Uighur, Kazakh, and Hui national minorities was also a very active religion up until the Cultural Revolution. A mosque I visited in Sian in 1966 served a community of 30,000 Hui, many of whom were still believers. They didn't eat pork and observed fasts such as Ramadan. Although the mosque was a Chinese style building, Arabic was the religious language. The mosque supported itself from collections and from the rent on houses it owned. However, because the building itself was a preserved site, the central government gave grants for its upkeep. There were three imams, one of whom had gone to Egypt in 1956. Five meetings were held each day and on Fridays some 200 to 300 people attended. This mosque was also closed down in 1966.

In many ways, the attacks of the Red guards appeared to indicate the end of freedom of religion in China. Neale Hunter summed up the situation in Shanghai.

Even though religion was in such a weak state, it came as a surprise in August 1966 when the Red Guards attacked it. In the major cities, the clergy were ordered to return to their native villages, the religious buildings were shorn of any architectural and ornamental features which the Red Guards found objectionable, anti-religious propaganda was put up on the walls, and every church, mosque, temple and monastery was 'secularised'. In Shanghai, Siccawei, the famous Catholic cathedral, lost its proud Gothic spires and became a fruit warehouse, at least one mosque was converted into offices, the International church and the Protestant cathedral were occu-occupied by Red Guard groups, and the Buddhist and Christian monasteries were emptied of their inhabitants and left deserted. Undoubtedly, these events severely disrupted the already declin-ing religious communities. However, after the Red Guard move-ment came to an end in 1968, overseas Chinese visiting their relatives reported that many Buddhist monasteries in the country-side were still operating more or less normally. By 1972, the Budd-hist Association was again functioning, though it was not repub-lishing its magazine. Two Americans who visited China met the head of the Association and visited temples in cities and in the countryside. The Xing Jiao Temple near Sian was an example of where 'there are still a small number of monks active and in contact with a small number of laymen; and . . . the latter carry on religious practices as long as these are clearly religious and kept at an individual level'. Apart from the obvious weakening of religious institutions in the cities, the situation had more or less reverted to that existing before 1966.

In 1974, Nikkei Niwano, a leading Japanese Buddhist, was invited to attend a joint meeting of the heads of the Chinese Buddhist, Christian, Islamic, and Taoist Associations. He was told that the Buddhists are now receiving assistance from the government for the rebuilding of temples destroyed during the Cultural Revolution. The Catholics said that they not changed their stand in accusing the Vatican of 'immoral conduct in work-ing for imperialism'. The Chinese Islamic Association told Niwano that they were playing a major role in strengthening friendly relations with Islamic States.

Clearly the Communist Party is not allowing this revival of religious activity because of any sympathy with its aims. There may be a feeling that the extreme methods of the Cultural Revolution were counterproductive, and that the religions can be expected to wither away as they were doing before 1966. Whatever the reasons, China's religious communities will remain weak and suspect, growing smaller as the old die off, and becoming increasingly remote from the rest of society.

The National Minorities

The Chinese call all those people living in China who are racially, linguistically, and culturally distinct from the 'Han' Chinese, who make up 95 per cent of the population, 'national minorities'. In the past these minority peoples were regarded with contempt. The old Chinese names for them implied that they were barbarians, little better than animals. Since 1949, the Communist Party has prided itself on changing this attitude. It has placed great emphasis on helping the minorities and preserving their cultures. As a result of these efforts, the Chinese government now officially recognises 54 separate minorities. Some, like the Manchus, have been so assimilated by the preponderant Hans as to be virtually indistinguishable. Others, like the Hui, are only counted as a separate race because of their continued adherence to Islam, the religion of their Arab ancestors. However, most are very different from the Hans in their cultures and ways of living.

In 1957, the national minority population of China was an estimated 38 million. Two thirds of these belonged to the 10 races with over 1 million members such as the Tibetans, Uighurs, Mongols, Miao, and Zhuang. The others ranged from the tiny group of 600 Hezhe in the far northeast, to those like the Yao, Dong, and Li each with several hundred thousand members living in groups dispersed throughout the southwestern provinces. Although the minority peoples only account for 5 per cent of the population, the areas they inhabit cover some 50 per cent of the whole country. Most of them live in the border regions, especially the large areas to the north and west that were not formally included in the Chinese state until the Qing rulers invaded them in the eighteenth century. Their integration into the Chinese state was often very tenuous before 1949. Although their land consists of inhospitable mountains, plateaus, deserts and steppelands, its strategic position along China's land frontiers make it very important to the central government.

Many of the national minorities share enough characteristics to be considered members of the same group of races under names like the Tibeto-Burmese, the Turkic, or the Zhuang-Thai. However, in practice there is great diversity in their cultures and in their historical relationships with the Chinese. Some, like the Uighurs and Kazakhs of Sinkiang, have cultural links with the Islamic world and affinities with peoples across the border in the Soviet Union. Others, like the Tibetans and Mongols have had an established social system of their own. Peoples like these have

64 *The products of the northeast underline the similarity of the environment with that across the border in the Soviet Union*

always been able to maintain some independence from the powerful and successful Chinese culture to the south. The smaller minorities, particularly those living in the hilly districts of the southern provinces, have not been so independent. They have always tended to absorb influences from their more advanced neighbours.

Although government policy towards the minorities has stressed their distinctness and the need to preserve their cultures, there has also been an undercurrent pressing for their reform and greater integration into Chinese society. Whenever these pressures have become strong, they have led to calls to sweep away minority religions, to restructure minority society immediately along Chinese lines, and to put an end to the remaining elements of national minority autonomy. However, in general the more gradual approach has been adopted. The minorities have been allowed greater latitude in the speed and nature of social reform. Often the pre-existing social leaders such as the lamas in Tibet or the village headmen of the southern tribes have been incorporated in the new political leadership. It was not until the late 1960s that the commune system of organisation became widespread in all the minority areas. Moreover the establishment of minority regions, districts, and counties with limited autonomy has meant that some consideration is always given to local customs and languages, and to promoting members of the minority races into the governmental and Party organisation. The Chinese thus see their work with the minorities as that of guiding them towards a new and better society. Nevertheless, old attitudes die hard and the Communists have often issued warnings against any feelings of 'Han superiority'. In 1961 some cadres working in Inner Mongolia were criticised for this:

> As most of the veteran cadres are Han Chinese ... they tend to look down upon or distrust Mongol cadres. They do not want to study the Mongolian language, they do not consider carefully the mentality and feeling of their Mongol comrades ... We must educate the Han Chinese, in particular the Han Chinese cadres, to ... respect the equal rights and opinions of national minorities and to eliminate the tendency towards the superior outlook of a big nationality ...

Until the Cultural Revolution, national minority affairs were dealt with jointly by the United Front Work Department of Party Central Committee and the Nationalities Affairs Commission of the State Council. In addition, the various government ministries and agencies also operated in minority areas, as did the Army with its large Production and Construction Corps in Sinkiang, and its garrison in Tibet. There have been no announcements of any reforms carried out during the Cultural Revolution. At the provincial level, there are five autonomous regions, the Sinkiang Uighur Autonomous Region, the Tibetan Autonomous Region, the Inner Mongolian Autonomous Region, the Ningsia Hui Autonomous Region, and the Kwangsi Zhuang Autonomous Region, together with many autonomous districts and counties. The purpose of these special arrangements is 'to guarantee political equality for the national minorities and to give special consideration to the characteristics of the minority areas so that the policies and principles of the Party and government can be implemented more effectively'. In practice, in their relationship with the central government, the minority regions function more or less in the same way as any other provinces or counties. Their limited powers of self-government basically allows them to make concessions to local cultures and languages, and to promote minority cadres. They may also draw up some regulations reflecting the local situation. For example, they may apportion electoral representation according to social conditions giving more power to traditional elites, and they may set up special governmental and tax collecting bodies. However, all these innovations have to be approved by the central government.

Under the general approach of recognising the 'special characteristics' of minority areas, the Chinese government has adopted a number of specific policies for minority areas. It has provided them with extra economic assistance and subsidies, developing their industries and communications and integrating them into the national economy. It has sent Han Chinese specialists out to give expert help and education. It has given the minority peoples equal political rights with all other Chinese, even to the extent of allowing them greater participation in the formal organs of government than their numbers justify. It has developed education in minority areas using the languages and scripts of the peoples themselves. It has also introduced scripts for those minorities that had not yet developed a written language. Minority culture has received publicity within China proper and touring troupes of Uighur and Mongol musicians are enthusiastically received. At the same time, the growing economic and social links between the outlying border regions and the Han Chinese has inevitably meant a growth in the use of Chinese words and institutions by the minorities.

Since the Party has generally aimed at obtaining popular voluntary acceptance of its policies among the minorities, a key target has been to train loyal minority cadres. In her essay 'Traditional Minorities Elites' (in R. A. Scalapino, *Elites in the People's Republic of China*), June Dreyer describes the ideal method of doing this put forward by the Party.

Tactics differed somewhat according to area, but in general the procedure was for the PLA to send in a work team to pay a call on the local leader. As the persons responsible for the fate of their communities vis-a-vis the outside world, headmen typically had had experience in dealing with outsiders as spokesmen for their respective groups . . .

If a headman was not disposed to cooperate, the work team would not force itself upon him, but would move on until it found a person more amenable to the group's presence. The team would then ask what the problems of the area were and suggest solutions. For example, if drought were mentioned, they might describe and offer to help build a small irrigation project. If it were malaria, drugs would be supplied and a plan outlined for killing mosquitoes and draining swamps. The work team would also try to find out local customs from the headman so as to avoid offending local sensitivities. Such gaucheries as sitting to the right of a campfire when custom dictated the left or preparing food in a manner considered unclean could prove major setbacks to the Party's good relations campaign.

While dispensing free seed, tools, labour, and entertainment, team members learned the local language and propagandised Party doctrine and Party nationalities policy. Minority individuals who appeared especially receptive to Communist propaganda and who gave evidence of leadership qualities might be singled out for special treatment, some being sent to a PLA-run cadre school in the area . . . Often people on the lowest rung of society were especially propagandised on the grounds that being the most exploited members of their groups, they would be particularly receptive to the Party's point of view . . . In this way, the Party aimed at gradually introducing reforms by working from within the minority group. However, as we have seen, many Hans still felt superior to the minorities and were unwilling to treat them as equals. In practice the ideal could be ignored, and either a policy of direct control of minorities or a laissez-faire attitude towards the original elites put in its place.

The diversity of traditional cultures and social structures has added to the problems facing the Chinese in their minority policy. The Uighurs speak a Turkic language and write with Arabic script. They are Mohammedans but also believe in a variety of ghosts and spirits. They practice both sedentary agriculture and nomadic sheep herding. In the past they tended to put loyalty to their immediate family above any wider considerations. By contrast, the Tibetans are Lama Buddhists and speak a language related to Burmese. Their written script is derived from that of Hindi. They do not have a strong national feeling and tend to divide themselves into tribes. Their diet of yak's meat, mutton, barley, flour, and tea is quite different from that of the Chinese to the east. In the past, their society was built around a strictly hierarchical nobility and priesthood. Serfdom was common and all political and economic power centred on the great monastries. The problem of working through and converting this traditional elite has been one of the most difficult problems the Chinese have

65 *The Yi minority—a mountain folk in Yuman Province*

faced. A further example of diversity is provided by the Miao people who live mainly in the province of Kweichow. This minority lives in scattered village communities, each with its own local characteristics. They practice a cut-and-burn form of agriculture in which the land is cleared by cutting and burning, farmed for a few years, and then new land is opened up. They usually farm in family groups. Their language is related to Chinese but has many dialect variations. Until 1949, political control was exercised by the village headmen. Their chief religion is shamanism with its mixture of gods, demons, ghosts, and ancestoral spirits. Inevitably, the Communist Party has had to develop different practical approaches to deal with each national minority.

Information on the feelings of the minorities themselves to-wards their present position is hard to come by. Some of the more primitive societies have probably lacked sufficient sense of national identity to want to achieve greater independence.

66 *A Tibetan militia
woman*

At the same time, they have benefitted materially from their contacts with the Chinese. Others like the Mongols and the Uighurs appear to have accepted their limited autonomy in return for improvements in their economic and social life. On the other hand, the Tibetans showed by their rebellion in 1959 that they were far from happy with the erosion of their traditional society. Undoubtedly the Tibetan nobles and Lamas played a leading role in attempting to maintain their power, but they did gain support from many of the fiercely independent tribesmen. The dilemma facing the Chinese was whether to countenance the continuation of a slave-owning society with great inequalities and cruelties in the hope that it could slowly develop in its own way, or whether to insist on some reforms even if it meant alienating many people. The choice was not an easy one, especially as the Chinese refused to accept any idea of national independence for the Tibetans. Furthermore, the problem was made more complicated by the role of foreign powers. Both the United States and India were implicated in Tibetan affairs and the Chinese were concerned to maintain the security of their border. Since that time, the Chinese have once again tried to use policies of cooperation and gradual development, though it is noticeable that Tibet is the region where there are the fewest national minority cadres working within the Party and government.

Ultimately, the problem of national security dominates much of China's national minority policy. The fact that most minorities live in regions along China's disputed frontiers with the Soviet Union and with India means that large numbers of Chinese troops have to be stationed in them. At the same time large numbers of Han Chinese have moved to live in Sinkiang and Inner Mongolia. These political pressures and movements of population, combined with the growing economic interdependence between China proper and its minority regions can only strengthen the integration of the minority peoples within the Chinese state.

Select Bibliography

General Studies

Donnithorne, A. *China's Economic System* (Allen and Unwin, 1967). A good introduction to all aspects of the Chinese economy.

Gittings, J. *A Chinese View of China* (BBC, 1973). A look at Chinese history and contemporary society through translations from Chinese authors.

Harrison, J. P. *The Long March to Power: A History of the Chinese Communist Party 1921–1972* (Macmillan 1972). A comprehensive survey of the history of the past 50 years relying on original and secondary sources.

Mao Tse-tung. *Selected Works* (Peking Foreign Languages Press). Mao's writings reflect the history of the Communist Party and the development of its ideology.

Schurmann, F. *Ideology and Organisation in Communist China* (University of California Press, 1968). A thorough analysis of the ideology of the Chinese Communist Party and its relationship to the political and social structure of the country.

Wilson, D. *A Quarter of Mankind* (Pelican, 1966). A useful survey of China on the eve of the Cultural Revolution.

The Communist Revolution

Belden, J. *China Shakes the World* (Pelican, 1973).

Johnson, C. *Peasant Nationalism and Communist Power* (Stanford University Press, 1962).

North, R. *Chinese Communism* (Weidenfeld and Nicolson, 1966).

Snow, E. *Red Star over China* (Gollancz, 1963).

Selden, M. *The Yenan Way in Revolutionary China* (Harvard University Press, 1972).

Politics

Doak Barnett, A. (ed.). *Chinese Communist Politics in Action* (University of Washington Press, 1969).

Doak Barnett, A. *Cadres, Bureaucracy, and Political Power in Communist China* (Columbia University Press, 1967). An account based on the information of former officials now living in Hong Kong.

Lifton, R. J. *Thought Reform and the Psychology of Totalism* (Penguin, 1967).

Liu, A. P. L. *Communications and National Integration in Communist China* (University of California Press, 1971).

Scalapino, R. A. *Elites in the People's Republic of China* (University of Washington Press, 1972).

Schram, S. *Mao Tse-tung* (Pelican, 1967).

Schram, S. (ed.). *Authority, Participation and Cultural Change in China* (Cambridge University Press, 1973).

Schram, S. (ed.), *Mao Tse-tung Unrehearsed* (Pelican, 1974).

Townsend, J. R. *Political Participation in Communist China* (University of California Press, 1967).

The Cultural Revolution

Ansley, C. *The Heresy of Wu Han* (University of Toronto Press, 1971).

Hinton, W. *Hundred Day War* (Monthly Review Press, 1972).

Hunter, N. *Shanghai Journal* (Praegar, 1969).

The Army

Cheng, J. C. *The Politics of the Chinese Red Army* (Hoover Institution Publications, Stanford, 1966).

Gittings, J. *The Role of the Chinese Army* (Oxford University Press, 1967).

Whitson, W. and Huang, C-h. *The Chinese Communist High Command: A History of Military Politics, 1927–1969* (Praegar, 1972).

The Economy

Chen, R. S. and Ridley, C. *Rural People's Communes in Lien-chiang* (Hoover Institution Press, 1969).

Buck, J. L. *Land Utilization in China* (Paragon Reprint, New York, 1968).

Feuerwerker, A. *The Chinese Economy 1912–1949* (Michigan, 1968).

Hinton, W. *Fanshen* (Pelican, 1972). An account of land reform.

Howe, C. *Employment and Economic Growth in Urban China 1949–1957* (Cambridge University Press, 1971).

Howe, C. *Wage Patterns and Policy in China 1919–1972* (Cambridge University Press, 1973).

Orleans, L. A. *Every Fifth Child: The Population of China* (Eyre Methuen, 1972).

Perkins, D. *Market Control and Planning in Communist China* (Harvard University Press, 1966).

Schran, P. *The Development of Chinese Agriculture 1950–1959* (University of Illinois Press, 1969).

Peking. *Socialist Upsurge in China's Countryside* (Peking Foreign Languages Press, 1957).

Tregear, T. R. *A Geography of China* (University of London Press, 1965).

U.S. Congress. *An Economic Profile of Mainland China* (Joint Economic Committee, U.S. Congress, Washington, 1967).

U.S. Congress. *People's Republic of China: An Economic Assessment* (Joint Economic Committee, U.S. Congress, 1972).

Walker, K. *Planning in Chinese Agriculture* (Cass, 1965).

The Countryside

Myrdal, J. *Report from a Chinese Village* (Pelican, 1967).

Yang, C. K. *A Chinese Village in Early Communist Transition* (Massachusetts Institute of Technology, 1959).

The City

Lewis, J. W. (ed.). *The City in Communist China* (Stanford University Press, 1971).

Murphey, R. *Shanghai Key to Modern China* (Harvard, 1953).

Vogel, E. *Canton under Communism* (Harvard, 1969).

The Family

Freedman, M. *Chinese Lineage and Society* (Athlone Press, 1966).

Freedman, M. (ed.). *Family and Kinship in Chinese Society* (Stanford, 1970).

Yang, C. K. *The Chinese Family in the Communist Revolution* (Massachusetts Institute of Technology, 1959).

Education and Culture

Fraser, S. *Chinese Communist Education: Records of the First Decade* (Vanderbilt University Press, 1965).

Goodman, M. *Literary Dissent in Communist China* (Harvard, 1967).

Hsia, C. T. *A History of Modern Chinese Fiction 1917–1957.*

Huang, J. C. *Heroes and Villains in Communist China* (C. Hurst and Co. London, 1973).

Klochko, M. *Soviet Scientist in China* (Hollis and Carter, London, 1964).

Orleans, L. A. *Professional Manpower and Education in Communist China* (National Science Foundation, U.S. Government, 1960).

Price, R. F. *Education in Communist China* (Routledge and Kegan Paul, London, 1970).

Ridley, C. P., Goodwin, P. H. and Doolin, D. J. *The Making of a Model Citizen in Communist China* (Standford, 1971).

Signer, E. and Galston, A. W. 'Education and Science in China', in *Science* (7 January 1972, Vol. 175, No. 4017).

Magazines

The China Quarterly. Published by the Contemporary China Institute of the School of Oriental and African Studies, London University. This journal contains articles on a wide variety of topics dealing with contemporary China. It also has regular book reviews and a chronicle of current events.

Summary of World Broadcasts Part Three. Published daily by the BBC Monitoring Service, this series carries translations of materials broadcast by the Chinese internal and external broadcasting services.

Chinese Literature. Published monthly in Peking, it has translations of modern literary works, reports on cultural events and illustrations by contemporary artists.

China Pictorial. Published monthly in Peking, pictures reflecting current events and news.

China Reconstructs. Published monthly in Peking, illustrated articles on China's economic and social development.

Peking Review. Published weekly in Peking, a political and current affairs magazine.

Index

The numerals in *italic type* refer to illustration numbers.